Better Homes and Gardens®

QUILT-LOVERS' FAVORITES®

FROM AMERICAN PATCHWORK & QUILTING®

Better Homes and Gardens® Creative Collection®
Des Moines, Iowa

VOLUME 11

Printing Number and Year: 5 4 3 2 1 04 03 02 01

ISBN: 978-0-696-30030-1

YOUR STORIES & REFLECTIONS

When you make a quilt, what you create is so much more than a covering—it is a reflection of you. In the pattern you select, the fabrics you choose, and most importantly, the time and talent you invest, your story is told. It's that legacy that guided our selection of projects to share with you in our latest edition, Volume 11, of Quilt-Lovers' Favorites®.

In this book you'll find 15 of our most popular patterns from past issues of American Patchwork & Quilting® *magazine and its sister publications. For a new twist on these favorite patterns, we present 30 all-new projects—quilts, pillows, a pincushion, table runners, and more—using the blocks, units, borders, or appliqué shapes from the original quilts. Color options add to the mix, showing how you can alter a pattern to reflect your style with different fabric and color combinations.*

To make the process easier, we include clear and concise instructions, full-size patterns, and a guide to quiltmaking basics—Quilter's Schoolhouse, page 157. *Our charts of optional sizes on the pattern pages will further help you customize your projects.*

The stories your quilts tell are uniquely yours. Dive in and discover patterns on the following pages that reflect your life, your loves, and your passion for quiltmaking. Enjoy!

Jennifer

Jennifer Erbe Keltner
Executive Editor, American Patchwork & Quilting

TABLE *of* CONTENTS

VINTAGE TREASURES

Page **6**

8 NANTUCKET STARS
- **13** Snowflakes Pillow
- **14** Four-Block Wall Quilt

16 FLYING SOLO
- **21** Zigzag Throw
- **24** Argyle Table Topper

26 SUMMER BREEZE
- **31** Red Zinger Throw
- **34** Floral Wall Quilt

ROTARY-CUT CHARMERS

Page **36**

38 CABIN COZY
- **44** Blue-and-White Log Cabins
- **46** Bear's Paw Message Board

48 WALLED GARDEN
- **52** Tranquil Breezes Quilt
- **55** Bountiful Harvest Throw

58 MIDNIGHT GARDEN
- **63** Strippy Solids Bed Quilt
- **66** All-Star Mini Quilt

PATTERN SHEET 2

- Optional Sizes Charts:
  - Nantucket Stars
  - Walled Garden
  - Midnight Garden
  - Ring of Fire
  - Color Cues
  - Modern Mix
  - Rhythm & Blues
  - Budding Beauty
- Coloring Diagrams
  - Flying Solo
  - Walled Garden
  - Pick & Choose

BOLD & BEAUTIFUL

Page **68**

70 RING OF FIRE
75 Seeing Spots Throw
77 Child's Play Quilt

80 COLOR CUES
84 Courtyard Throw
86 Photo Wall Quilt

88 COLOR BURST
93 Red Delicious
96 Flying Geese Pot Holders

FUN WITH FAT QUARTERS

Page **98**

100 PICK & CHOOSE
106 Polka-Dot Apron
108 Shades of the Sea Throw

110 MODERN MIX
115 Me and My Shadow
117 Raspberry-Limeade Table Topper

120 RHYTHM & BLUES
125 Flannel Kid's Quilt
127 Farmer's Market Table Mat

APPLIQUÉ YOUR WAY

Page **128**

130 BUDDING BEAUTY
136 Sunflower Table Runner
138 Blooming Pincushion

140 BIRDS OF A FEATHER
144 All in the Family Pillow
146 Grandma's Little Birdies

148 ARTFULLY INSPIRED
152 Falling Leaves
155 Circles Sewing Bag

157 QUILTER'S SCHOOLHOUSE
157 Choose Fabrics
Cut Bias Strips
Make and Use Templates
Piecing
158 Set in Pieces
159 Miter Borders
Complete Quilt

160 CREDITS

VINTAGE TREASURES

Quiltmakers have always used fabric scraps to create quilts. The variety of color and design continue to inspire quiltmakers decades after the quilts are completed. Use reproduction prints to make similar versions of the antique quilts featured in this chapter, or substitute contemporary prints to create heirlooms all your own.

21
8
16
34

NANTUCKET *Stars*

This 1860s quilt from collector Miraim Kujac reveals its character in the block's name—Old Maid's Patience. Take your time with this set-in-seams treasure. It's worth the wait.

Materials

1 yard total assorted red prints (blocks)

3/8 yard total assorted blue prints (blocks)

1 yard total assorted black prints (blocks)

1/4 yard total assorted green prints (blocks)

5/8 yard total assorted cream prints (blocks)

1/4 yard total assorted tan prints (blocks)

2½ yards cream pin dot (blocks)

½ yard solid Cheddar (blocks)

4¼ yards muslin (setting squares, setting and corner triangles, binding)

7⅞ yards backing fabric

94" square batting

Finished quilt: 85⅜" square
Finished block: 12" square

Quantities are for 44/45"-wide, 100% cotton fabrics. **Measurements** include ¼" seam allowances. Sew with right sides together unless otherwise stated.

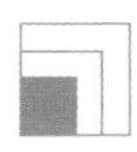

SIZE OPTIONS: For a chart of optional sizes, turn to *Pattern Sheet 2*.

Cut Fabrics

Cut pieces in the following order. The Diamond Pattern is on *Pattern Sheet 1*. To make a template of the pattern, see Make and Use Templates, *page 157*. Be sure to transfer dots marked on pattern to template, then to fabric pieces. These dots are matching points and are necessary when joining pieces.

From assorted red prints, cut:
- 256 of Diamond Pattern (16 sets of 16 matching diamonds)

From assorted blue prints, cut:
- 64 of Diamond Pattern (4 sets of 16 matching diamonds)

From assorted black prints, cut:
- 240 of Diamond Pattern (15 sets of 16 matching diamonds)

From assorted green prints, cut:
- 48 of Diamond Pattern (3 sets of 16 matching diamonds)

From assorted cream prints, cut:
- 144 of Diamond Pattern (9 sets of 16 matching diamonds)

From assorted tan prints, cut:
- 48 of Diamond Pattern (3 sets of 16 matching diamonds)

From cream pin dot, cut:
- 25—4" squares
- 100—2¼×4" rectangles

continued

- 50—3¾" squares, cutting each diagonally twice in an X for 200 triangles total
- 100—2¼" squares

From solid Cheddar, cut:
- 100—2¼" squares

From muslin, cut:
- 9—2½×42" binding strips
- 4—18¼" squares, cutting each diagonally twice in an X for 16 setting triangles total
- 16—12½" setting squares
- 2—9⅜" squares, cutting each in half diagonally for 4 corner triangles total

Assemble Units

We recommend hand-piecing the star units and blocks because so many pieces must be set in. If you wish to machine-piece, be sure to start and end at the dots when indicated in the assembly instructions.

As you piece the star units, finger-press seams in the desired direction to help keep your work smooth. Trim points to reduce bulk. Press completed units and finished quilt top with an iron, pressing seams in the directions that allow them to lie as flat as possible or that will enable you to quilt as desired without stitching through seam allowances.

1. For star units in one block you'll need: 16 matching diamonds from one print, 16 matching diamonds from a second print, eight cream pin dot triangles, and four cream pin dot 2¼" squares.

2. Pin together a diamond from each print, carefully aligning seam allowances and matching points. (To align matching points, place a pin through each marked dot.) Sew together to make a diamond pair, making sure you do not stitch into ¼" seam allowance at inner corner (blue dot on **Diagram 1**). Press seam toward darker print. Repeat to make 16 diamond pairs total.

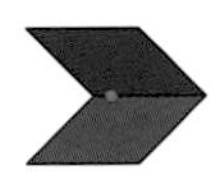
Diagram 1

3. Pin a cream pin dot triangle to one diamond in a diamond pair; the triangle will extend slightly beyond outer point of diamond. Sew from inner corner (blue dot on **Diagram 2**) to outside corner. Bring up adjacent diamond in pair and pin to cream pin dot triangle. Stitch from inner corner to outside corner as before to make a star point unit. Press all seams toward diamonds. (For details, see Set In Pieces, *page 158*.) Repeat to make eight star point units total (you'll have eight diamond pairs remaining).

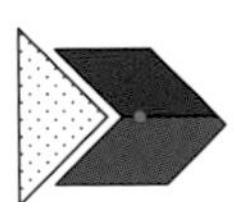
Diagram 2

4. Join two star point units, making sure you don't stitch into ¼" seam allowance at inner corner. Press seam toward darker print. Set a cream pin dot 2¼" square into inner corner to make a star corner unit; square will extend slightly beyond outer edges of diamond points **(Diagram 3).** Press seams toward diamonds. Repeat to make four star corner units total.

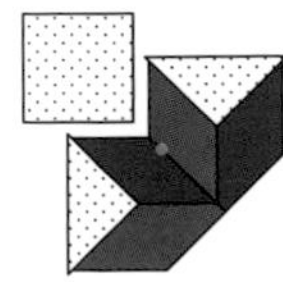
Diagram 3

5. Join two remaining diamond pairs to make a star half, making sure you don't stitch into ¼" seam allowance at inner corner. Press seam toward darker print. Sew together a star corner unit and the star half to make a star unit; do not stitch into either ¼" seam allowance **(Diagram 4).** Press seam in one direction. Repeat to make four star units total.

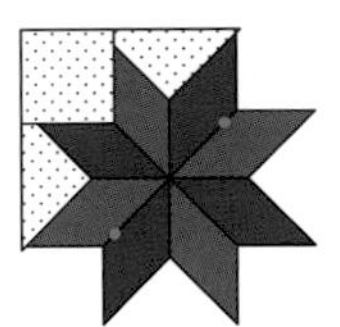
Diagram 4

6. Repeat steps 1–5 to make 100 star units total (25 sets of four matching star units).

Assemble Blocks

1. Referring to **Block Assembly Diagram,** lay out four matching star units, four cream pin dot 2¼×4" rectangles, four solid Cheddar 2¼" squares, and a cream pin dot 4" square.

Block Assembly Diagram

2. Sew together pieces in segments, working from upper edge of block to lower edge, to make a block. Stitch from inner corner to outside corner as before, making sure you don't stitch into ¼" seam allowance. (Our quilt tester first set in the solid Cheddar squares, then the cream pin dot rectangles, and finally the cream pin dot square.) Press seams toward solid Cheddar and cream pin dot pieces. The block should be 12½" square including seam allowances.

3. Repeat steps 1 and 2 to make 25 blocks total.

continued

Quilting Diagram

Assemble Quilt Top

1. Referring to **Quilt Assembly Diagram**, lay out blocks, muslin setting squares, and muslin setting triangles in nine diagonal rows.

2. Sew together pieces in each row. Press seams toward setting pieces.

3. Join rows; press seams in one direction. Add muslin corner triangles to complete quilt top. Press seams toward corner triangles.

Finish Quilt

1. Layer quilt top, batting, and backing; baste. (For details, see Complete Quilt, *page 159*.)

2. Quilt as desired. On this antique quilt, a 1¾" vertical and diagonal hand-quilted grid fills the setting squares and triangles, and each block is outline-quilted **(Quilting Diagram)**.

3. Bind with muslin binding strips. (For details, see Complete Quilt.)

Quilt Assembly Diagram

SNOWFLAKES PILLOW

Make a festive wintertime pillow using just one block.

Materials

$\frac{5}{8}$ yard white snowflake print (block, border, pillow back)

$\frac{1}{8}$ yard red print (block)

4—$\frac{3}{4}$"-diameter buttons: red

16"-square pillow form *or* polyester fiberfill

Finished pillow: 16" square

Cut Fabrics

Cut pieces in the following order. This project uses *Nantucket Stars* Diamond Pattern on *Pattern Sheet 1.*

From white snowflake print, cut:

- 1—16½" pillow back square
- 2—2½×16½" border strips
- 2—2½×12½" border strips
- 32 of Diamond Pattern

From red print, cut:

- 1—4" square
- 4—2¼×4" rectangles
- 2—3¾" squares, cutting each diagonally twice in an X for 8 triangles total
- 8—2¼" squares

Assemble Block

1. Referring to Assemble Units, steps 2–5, *page 11,* and photo, *above right,* use white snowflake print diamond pieces, red print triangles, and four red print 2¼" squares to make four star units total.

2. Referring to Assemble Blocks, steps 1 and 2, *page 11,* and photo, use star units and remaining red print pieces to make a block.

Finish Pillow

1. Sew short white snowflake print border strips to opposite edges of block. Add long white snowflake print border strips to remaining edges to complete pillow top. Press all seams toward border.

2. Referring to photo, *above,* hand-stitch a button to center of each star unit.

3. Layer pillow top and white snowflake print 16½" pillow back square with right sides together. Sew together to make pillow cover, leaving an opening along one edge for turning.

4. Turn pillow cover right side out; insert pillow form or stuff with fiberfill. Hand-stitch opening closed.

FOUR-BLOCK WALL QUILT

Large setting squares provide a backdrop for beautiful machine quilting.

Materials

- 3⁄8 yard total assorted blue prints (blocks, binding)
- 1⁄4 yard total assorted brown prints (blocks)
- 3⁄8 yard total assorted green prints (blocks, binding)
- 4—1⁄8-yard pieces assorted light prints in cream, green, and ivory (blocks)
- 1⁄8 yard solid cream (blocks)
- 7⁄8 yard green tone-on-tone (setting squares, setting and corner triangles)
- 1⁄2 yard brown floral (border)
- 2 5⁄8 yards backing fabric
- 47" square batting

Finished quilt:
38½" square

Cut Fabrics

Cut pieces in the following order.

This project uses *Nantucket Stars* Diamond Pattern on *Pattern Sheet 1.*

From assorted blue prints, cut:
- 2—2½×42" binding strips
- 48 of Diamond Pattern (3 sets of 16 matching diamonds)

From assorted brown prints, cut:
- 48 of Diamond Pattern (3 sets of 16 matching diamonds)

From assorted green prints, cut:
- 2—2½×42" binding strips
- 32 of Diamond Pattern (2 sets of 16 matching diamonds)

From *each* assorted light print, cut:
- 1—4" square
- 4—2¼×4" rectangles
- 2—3¾" squares, cutting each diagonally twice in an X for 8 triangles total
- 4—2¼" squares

From solid cream, cut:
- 16—2¼" squares

From green tone-on-tone, cut:
- 1—18¼" square, cutting it diagonally twice in an X for 4 setting triangles total
- 1—12½" setting square
- 2—9⅜" squares, cutting each in half diagonally for 4 corner triangles total

From brown floral, cut:
- 2—2½×38½" border strips
- 2—2½×34½" border strips

Assemble Blocks

1. For one block you'll need: 16 matching diamonds from one print; 16 matching diamonds from a second print; pieces from one light print (one 4" square, four 2¼×4" rectangles, eight triangles, and four 2¼" squares); and four solid cream 2¼" squares.

2. Referring to Assemble Units, steps 2–5, *page 11,* and photo, *opposite,* use diamonds, light print triangles, and light print 2¼" squares to make four matching star units total.

3. Referring to Assemble Blocks, steps 1 and 2, *page 11,* and photo, *opposite,* use matching star units, solid cream 2¼" squares, and light print 2¼×4" rectangles and 4" square to make a block.

4. Repeat steps 1–3 to make four blocks total.

Assemble Quilt Top

1. Referring to **Quilt Assembly Diagram,** lay out blocks, green tone-on-tone setting square, and green tone-on-tone setting triangles in three diagonal rows.

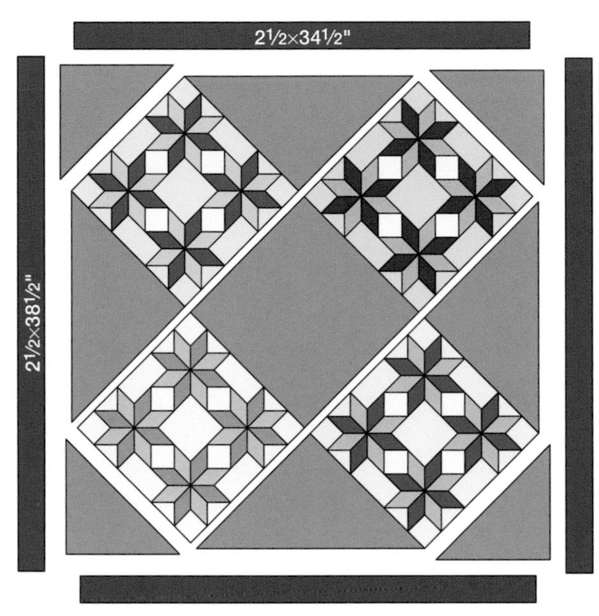

Quilt Assembly Diagram

2. Sew together pieces in each row. Press seams toward setting pieces.

3. Join rows; press seams in one direction. Add green tone-on-tone corner triangles to complete quilt center. Press seams toward corner triangles. The quilt center should be 34½" square including seam allowances.

4. Sew short brown floral border strips to opposite edges of quilt center. Add long brown floral border strips to remaining edges to complete quilt top. Press all seams toward border.

Finish Quilt

1. Layer quilt top, batting, and backing; baste. (For details, see Complete Quilt, *page 159.*)

2. Quilt as desired. A feathered floral design with an eight-pointed star in the center is machine-quilted on the setting square and setting triangles of the featured quilt.

3. Using diagonal seams, join assorted blue and green print 2½×42" binding strips to make a pieced binding strip. Bind quilt with pieced binding strip. (For details, see Complete Quilt.)

FLYING *Solo*

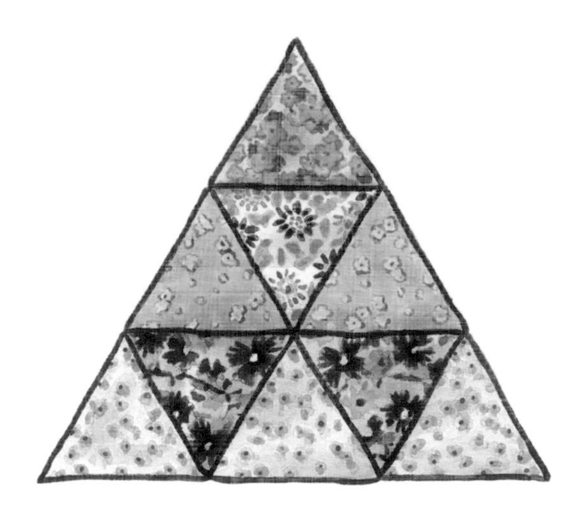

A triangle is the only shape needed to re-create the center of this vintage quilt from the collection of Julie Hendricksen. Points of the equilateral triangles match up perfectly, making stitching a breeze.

Materials

4 yards total *or* 12—¼-yard pieces assorted dark prints and solids (rows, binding)

4 yards total *or* 12—¼-yard pieces assorted light prints and solids (rows, binding)

2½ yards solid purple (border)

5 yards backing fabric

80×92" batting

Finished quilt: 72×83¾"

Quantities are for 44/45"-wide, 100% cotton fabrics. **Measurements** include ¼" seam allowances. Sew with right sides together unless otherwise stated.

Cut Fabrics

Cut pieces in the following order.

Patterns are on *Pattern Sheet 1.* To make templates of patterns, see Make and Use Templates, *page 157.* Be sure to transfer dots marked on patterns to templates, then to fabric pieces. These dots are matching points and are necessary when joining pieces.

The diagonal rows of this antique quilt consist of alternating light and dark triangles. To duplicate this look, arrange your fabrics in pairs of lights and darks before cutting.

Combine rotary cutting and templates for quick, accurate A triangles. Rotary-cut 4×42" strips, then use the A template to cut A triangles across the fabric width **(Cutting Diagram).** Or use an acrylic template made specifically for cutting 60° triangles.

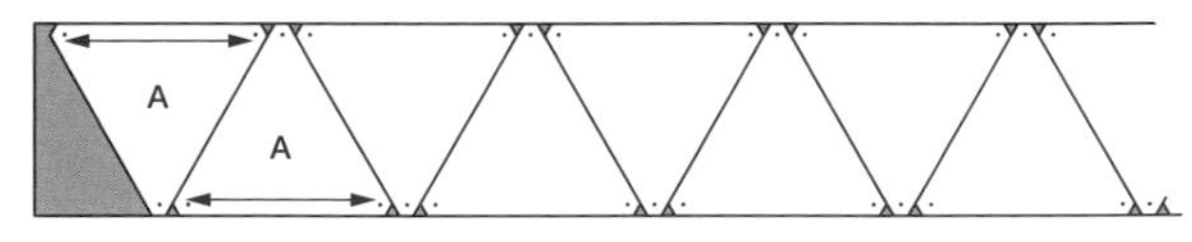

Cutting Diagram

Cut A, B, and C triangles for each row as indicated below and on **Quilt Assembly Diagram** on *page 19.* After cutting triangles for a row, organize them in a resealable bag marked with the row number.

Row 1:
- 1 dark Pattern A
- 1 dark Pattern C
- 1 light Pattern B

Row 2:
- 2 dark Pattern A
- 1 dark Pattern B
- 3 light Pattern A
- 1 light Pattern C

Row 3:
- 4 dark Pattern A
- 1 dark Pattern B
- 5 light Pattern A
- 1 light Pattern C

Row 4:
- 6 dark Pattern A
- 1 dark Pattern B
- 7 light Pattern A
- 1 light Pattern C

continued

Row 5:
- 8 dark Pattern A
- 1 dark Pattern B
- 9 light Pattern A
- 1 light Pattern C

Row 6:
- 10 dark Pattern A
- 1 dark Pattern B
- 11 light Pattern A
- 1 light Pattern C

Row 7:
- 12 dark Pattern A
- 1 dark Pattern B
- 13 light Pattern A
- 1 light Pattern C

Row 8:
- 14 dark Pattern A
- 1 dark Pattern B
- 15 light Pattern A
- 1 light Pattern C

Row 9:
- 16 dark Pattern A
- 1 dark Pattern B
- 17 light Pattern A
- 1 light Pattern C

Rows 10–18 *each:*
- 18 dark Pattern A
- 18 light Pattern A

Row 19:
- 18 dark Pattern A
- 17 light Pattern A
- 1 light Pattern B

Row 20:
- 16 dark Pattern A
- 1 dark Pattern C
- 15 light Pattern A
- 1 light Pattern B

Row 21:
- 14 dark Pattern A
- 1 dark Pattern C
- 13 light Pattern A
- 1 light Pattern B

Row 22:
- 12 dark Pattern A
- 1 dark Pattern C
- 11 light Pattern A
- 1 light Pattern B

Row 23:
- 10 dark Pattern A
- 1 dark Pattern C
- 9 light Pattern A
- 1 light Pattern B

Row 24:
- 8 dark Pattern A
- 1 dark Pattern C
- 7 light Pattern A
- 1 light Pattern B

Row 25:
- 6 dark Pattern A
- 1 dark Pattern C
- 5 light Pattern A
- 1 light Pattern B

Row 26:
- 4 dark Pattern A
- 1 dark Pattern C
- 3 light Pattern A
- 1 light Pattern B

Row 27:
- 2 dark Pattern A
- 1 dark Pattern C
- 1 light Pattern A
- 1 light Pattern B

Row 28:
- 1 dark Pattern C

From solid purple, cut:
- 8—4¾×42" strips for border

From remaining assorted dark and light prints and solids, cut:
- Enough 2½"-wide strips in lengths ranging from 4" to 9" to total 340" in length for binding

Assemble Quilt Center

1. Referring to **Quilt Assembly Diagram**, lay out A, B, and C triangles in diagonal rows.

continued

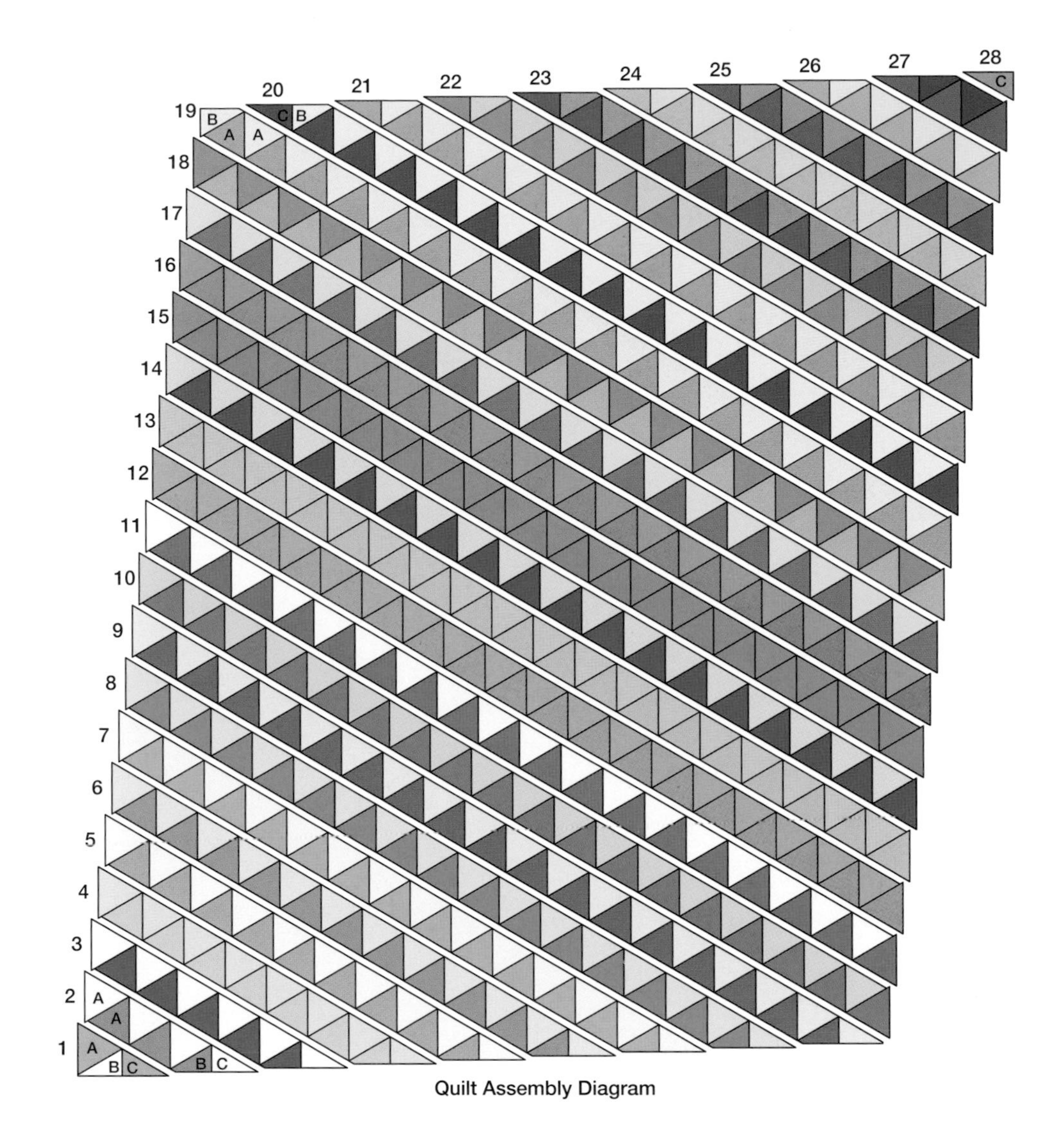

Quilt Assembly Diagram

Binding Details

Put the final touch on a scrappy quilt with a binding pieced from the same fabrics as the quilt center. A pieced binding is especially striking when paired with a solid color, such as the solid purple border featured in *Flying Solo*.

For different looks, experiment with how you piece your binding strips—diagonal or straight seams. To reduce bulk, press seams open and consider using a single-fold binding instead of a French-fold (or double-fold) method.

2. Aligning marked matching points, sew together pieces in each row. Sew bias edges of triangles together, keeping grain line of triangles along the long edges of each diagonal row. Doing so will minimize stretching and make joining rows easier. Press seams in one direction, alternating direction with each row.

3. Join rows to make quilt center; press seams in one direction. The quilt center should be 63½×75¼" including seam allowances.

Add Border

1. Cut and piece solid purple 4¾×42" strips to make:

- 2—4¾×88" border strips
- 2—4¾×76" border strips

2. With midpoints aligned, sew long border strips to long edges of quilt center, beginning and ending seams ¼" from quilt center edges. Press seams toward border.

3. Add short border strips to remaining edges, mitering corners, to complete quilt top. (For details, see Miter Borders, *page 159*). Press seams toward border.

Finish Quilt

1. Layer quilt top, batting, and backing; baste. (For details, see Complete Quilt, *page 159.*)

Quilting Diagram

2. Quilt as desired. The quilter of this antique piece hand-stitched a diamond grid that follows the lines of the triangle pieces; grid lines are spaced 1" apart. A diamond chain fills the border **(Quilting Diagram).**

3. Using straight seams, sew together assorted dark and light print and solid binding strips to make a pieced binding strip. Bind quilt with pieced binding strip. (For details, see Complete Quilt.)

optional colors

Stripes vs. Solids

Instead of varying the triangles in each row by lights and darks, quilt tester Laura Boehnke alternated between soft stripes and heathered solids.

"Although my interpretation of *Flying Solo* has a slightly modern look, the colors are so soft and livable, I think many people could still imagine it in their homes," Laura says. A 2"-wide-finished border is the right scale for this small table runner.

ZIGZAG THROW

Careful placement of light and dark prints creates a zigzag effect.

Materials

2½ yards total *or* 20—9×22" pieces (fat eighths) assorted medium and dark prints (rows, binding)

2½ yards total *or* 20—9×22" pieces (fat eighths) assorted light prints (rows, binding)

3½ yards backing fabric

63×65" batting

Finished quilt: 55×56½"

Cut Fabrics

Cut pieces in the following order.

This project uses *Flying Solo* patterns A and C on *Pattern Sheet 1.*

From assorted medium and dark prints, cut:
- 208 of Pattern A
- 16 of Pattern C

From assorted light prints, cut:
- 208 of Pattern A
- 16 of Pattern C

From remaining assorted medium, dark, and light prints, cut:
- Enough 2½"-wide strips in lengths ranging from 10" to 21" to total 260" in length for binding

Assemble Quilt Top

1. Referring to **Quilt Assembly Diagram**, lay out A and C triangles in 16 horizontal rows, alternating assorted light prints with assorted medium and dark prints.

2. Aligning marked matching points, sew together pieces in each row. Sew bias edges of triangles together, keeping grain line of triangles along the

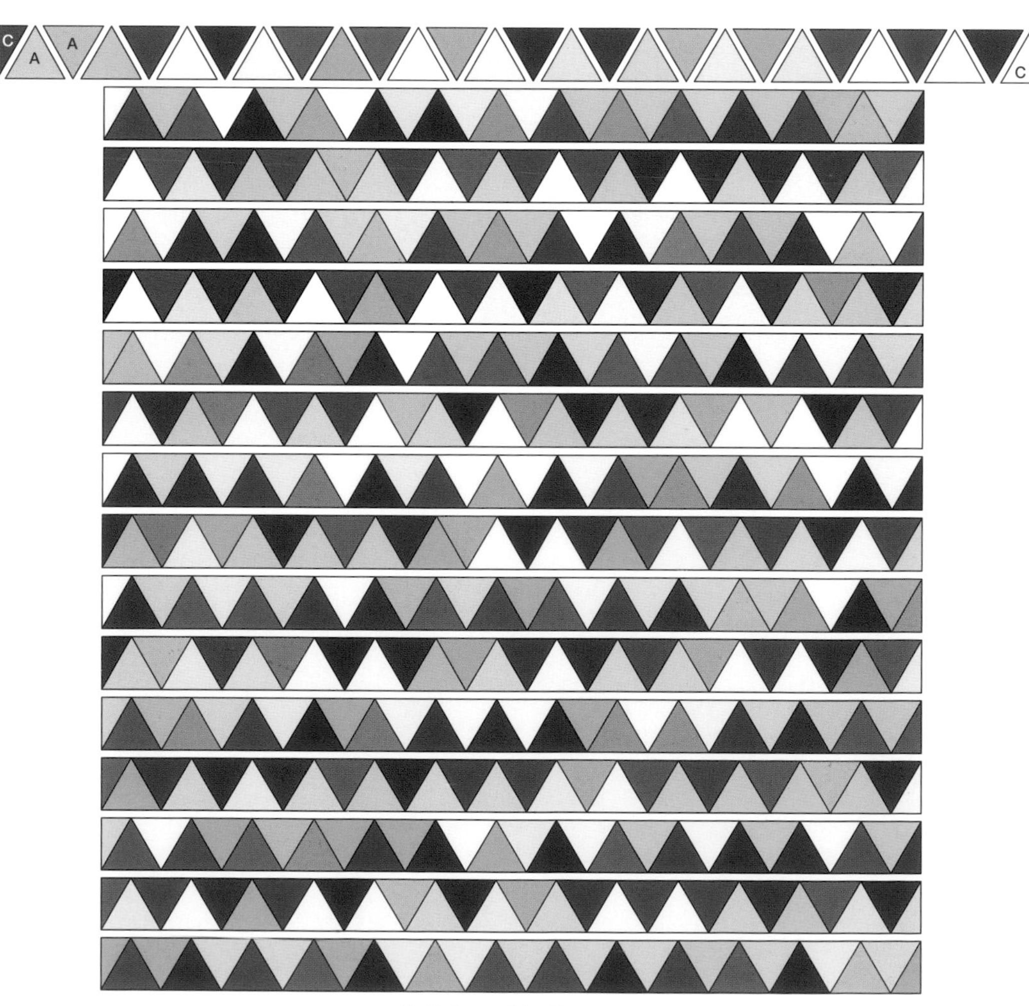

Quilt Assembly Diagram

long edges of each horizontal row. Press seams in one direction.

3. Join rows to complete quilt top; press seams in one direction.

Finish Quilt

1. Layer quilt top, batting, and backing; baste. (For details, see Complete Quilt, *page 159*.)

2. Quilt as desired. A continuous leaf and vine motif is stitched across the quilt top.

3. Using diagonal seams, join assorted medium, dark, and light print binding strips to make a pieced binding strip. Bind quilt with pieced binding strip. (For details, see Complete Quilt.)

ARGYLE TABLE TOPPER

There is no trick to creating this sophisticated Halloween treat. Simply arrange triangles of the same prints next to each other to form diamonds.

Materials

⅛ yard *each* of cream print No. 1 and cream print No. 2 (rows)

¼ yard *each* of orange print No. 1 and orange print No. 2 (rows)

¼ yard black print No. 1 (rows)

¼ yard black print No. 2 (inner border)

⅜ yard cream print No. 3 (outer border)

⅜ yard black tone-on-tone (binding)

1¼ yards backing fabric

32×44" batting

Finished table runner: 23⅝×35½"

Cut Fabrics

Cut pieces in the following order.

This project uses *Flying Solo* patterns on *Pattern Sheet 1*.

From *each* cream print No. 1 and No. 2, cut:

- 8 of Pattern A

From *each* orange print No. 1 and No. 2, cut:

- 12 of Pattern A
- 4 of Pattern B
- 4 of Pattern C

From black print No. 1, cut:

- 16 of Pattern A

From black print No. 2, cut:

- 2—1½×28½" inner border strips
- 2—1½×18⅝" inner border strips

From cream print No. 3, cut:

- 2—3×30½" outer border strips
- 2—3×23¾" outer border strips

From black tone-on-tone, cut:

- 3—2½×42" binding strips

Assemble Table Runner Center

1. Referring to **Table Runner Assembly Diagram**, lay out A, B, and C triangles in eight horizontal rows, placing matching prints next to each other as shown.

2. Aligning marked matching points, sew together pieces in each row. Press seams in one direction.

3. Join rows to make table runner center; press seams in one direction. The table runner center should be 16¾×28½" including seam allowances.

Add Borders

1. Join long black print No. 2 inner border strips to long edges of table runner center. Add short black print No. 2 inner border strips to remaining edges. Press all seams toward inner border.

2. Sew long cream print No. 3 outer border strips to long edges of table runner center. Join short cream print No. 3 outer border strips to remaining edges to complete table runner top. Press all seams toward outer border.

Finish Table Runner

1. Layer table runner top, batting, and backing; baste. (For details, see Complete Quilt, *page 159*.)

2. Quilt as desired. The featured quilt is stitched in the ditch.

3. Bind with black tone-on-tone binding strips. (For details, see Complete Quilt.)

Table Runner Assembly Diagram

SUMMER *Breeze*

This vintage throw from quilt collector Julie Hendricksen features a large selection of fabrics from the 1930s.

Materials

3¼ yards total assorted 1930s prints (blocks, outer border)

3⅔ yards muslin (blocks; inner, middle, and outer borders)

1½ yards solid blue (blocks, inner and outer borders, binding)

5 yards backing fabric

89×84" batting

Finished quilt: 81×75¼"
Finished blocks: 10½" square

Quantities are for 44/45"-wide, 100% cotton fabrics. **Measurements** include ¼" seam allowances. Sew with right sides together unless otherwise stated.

Cut Fabrics

Cut pieces in the following order.

From assorted 1930s prints, cut:
- 100—2½" squares
- 936—2" squares

From muslin, cut:
- 2—8×42" strips for inner border
- 4—4⅞×42" strips for middle border
- 4—2×42" strips for middle border
- 18—8" squares
- 72—2×5" rectangles
- 48—4⅛" squares, cutting each diagonally twice in an X for 192 large triangles total
- 16—2⅜" squares, cutting each in half diagonally for 32 small triangles total

From solid blue, cut:
- 8—2½×42" binding strips
- 4—2×42" strips for inner border
- 4—2½" squares
- 166—2" squares

Assemble A Blocks

1. Referring to **Diagram 1**, sew assorted 1930s print 2" squares to opposite ends of a muslin 2×5" rectangle to make a small pieced rectangle. Press seams toward 1930s prints. Repeat to make 72 small pieced rectangles total.

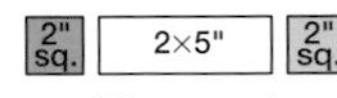

Diagram 1

2. Sew solid blue 2" squares to opposite ends of a small pieced rectangle to make a large pieced rectangle **(Diagram 2)**. Press seams toward solid blue. Repeat to make 36 large pieced rectangles total.

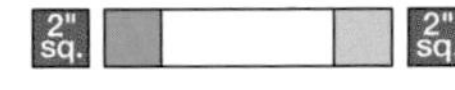

Diagram 2

continued

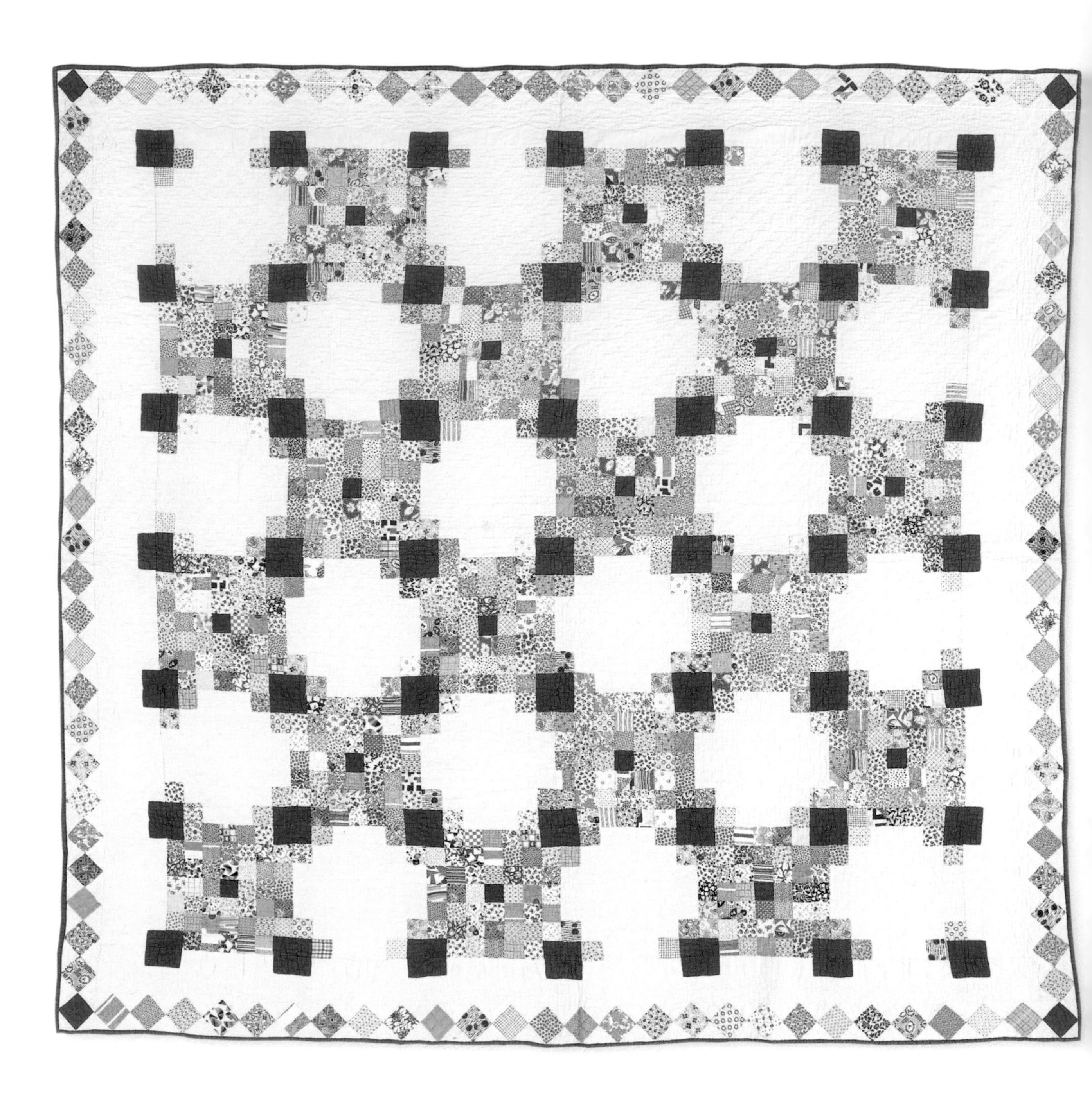

3. Referring to **Diagram 3**, sew small pieced rectangles to opposite edges of a muslin 8" square. Press seams toward muslin square.

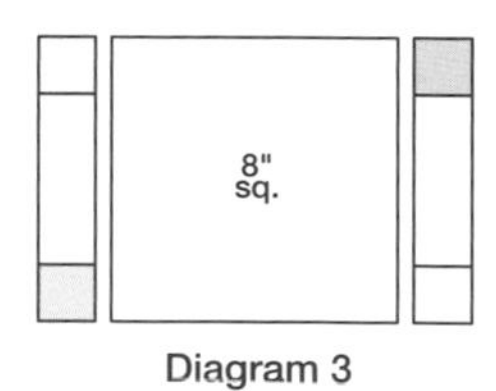

Diagram 3

4. Sew large pieced rectangles to remaining edges of muslin 8" square to make an A block **(Diagram 4).** Press seams toward muslin square. The block should be 11" square including seam allowances.

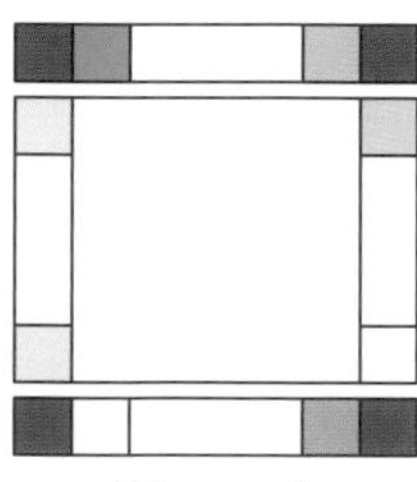
Diagram 4

5. Repeat steps 3 and 4 to make 18 A blocks total.

Assemble B Blocks

1. Referring to **Diagram 5**, lay out five solid blue 2" squares and 44 assorted 1930s print 2" squares in seven horizontal rows.

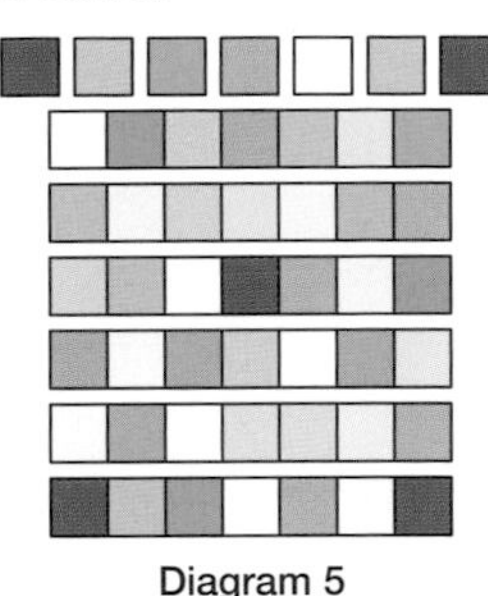

Diagram 5

2. Sew together squares in each row. Press seams in one direction, alternating direction with each row.

3. Join rows to make a B block. Press seams in one direction. The block should be 11" square including seam allowances.

4. Repeat steps 1–3 to make 18 B blocks total.

Assemble Quilt Center

1. Referring to **Diagram 6** and **Quilt Assembly Diagram** on *page 30,* lay out A and B blocks in six rows.

A	B	A	B	A	B
B	A	B	A	B	A
A	B	A	B	A	B
B	A	B	A	B	A
A	B	A	B	A	B
B	A	B	A	B	A

Diagram 6

2. Sew together blocks in each row; press seams in one direction, alternating direction with each row. Join rows to make quilt center. Press seams in one direction. The quilt center should be 63½" square including seam allowances.

Assemble and Add Inner Border

1. Referring to **Diagram 7**, sew together two solid blue 2×42" strips and one muslin 8×42" strip to make a strip set. Press seams toward solid blue strips. Repeat to make a second strip set.

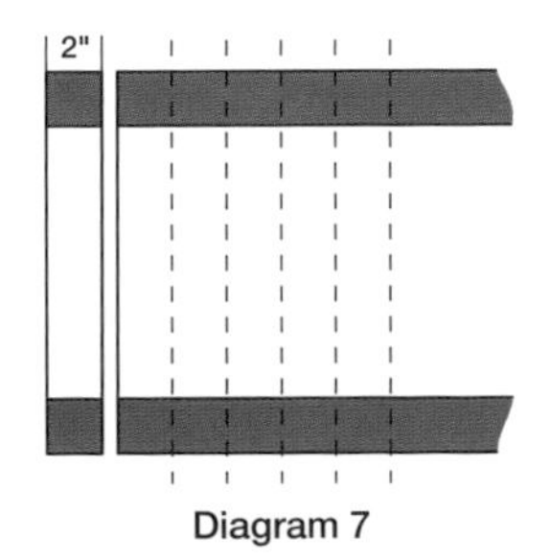

Diagram 7

2. Cut strip sets into 24—2"-wide segments total.

3. Join six 2"-wide segments to make a short inner border strip (**Quilt Assembly Diagram** on *page 30*). Press seams in one direction. The short inner border strip should be 2×63½" including seam allowances. Repeat to make a second short inner border strip.

4. Sew together six 2"-wide segments and two solid blue 2" squares to make a long inner border strip **(Quilt Assembly Diagram).** Press seams in one direction. The long inner border strip should be 2×66½" including seam allowances. Repeat to make a second long inner border strip.

5. Sew short inner border strips to opposite edges of quilt center. Add long inner border strips to remaining edges. Press all seams toward border.

Add Middle Border

1. Cut and piece muslin 4⅞×42" strips to make:
- 2—4⅞×66½" middle border strips

2. Cut and piece muslin 2×42" strips to make:
- 2—2×75¼" middle border strips

3. Referring to **Quilt Assembly Diagram** on *page 30*, sew short middle border strips to opposite edges of quilt center. Add long middle border strips to remaining edges. Press all seams toward middle border.

Assemble and Add Outer Border

1. Sew muslin large triangles to opposite edges of a 1930s print 2½" square to make unit A **(Diagram 8).** Press seams toward triangles. Repeat to make 92 A units total.

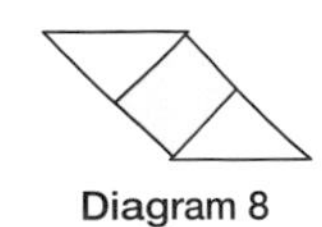

Diagram 8

2. Referring to **Diagram 9**, join a muslin large triangle and a muslin small triangle to opposite edges of a 1930s print 2½" square; press seams toward triangles. Add a second muslin small triangle to make unit B. Press seam toward triangle. Repeat to make eight B units total.

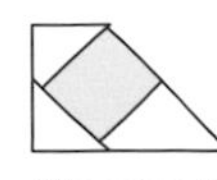

Diagram 9

continued

3. Sew muslin small triangles to opposite edges of a solid blue 2½" square **(Diagram 10).** Press seams toward triangles. Add muslin small triangles to remaining edges to make a Square-in-a-Square unit. Press seams toward triangles. The unit should be 3⅜" square including seam allowances. Repeat to make four Square-in-a-Square units total.

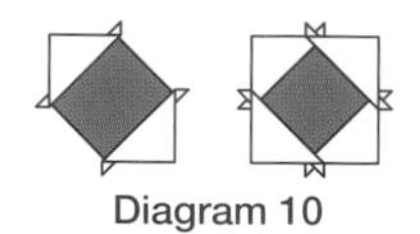
Diagram 10

4. Carefully matching seams, sew together 22 A units and two B units to make a short outer border strip **(Quilt Assembly Diagram).** Press seams in one direction. The short outer border strip should be 3⅜×69½" including seam allowances. Repeat to make a second short outer border strip.

5. Join 24 A units and two B units in a row **(Quilt Assembly Diagram).** Add a Square-in-a-Square unit to each end of row to make a long outer border

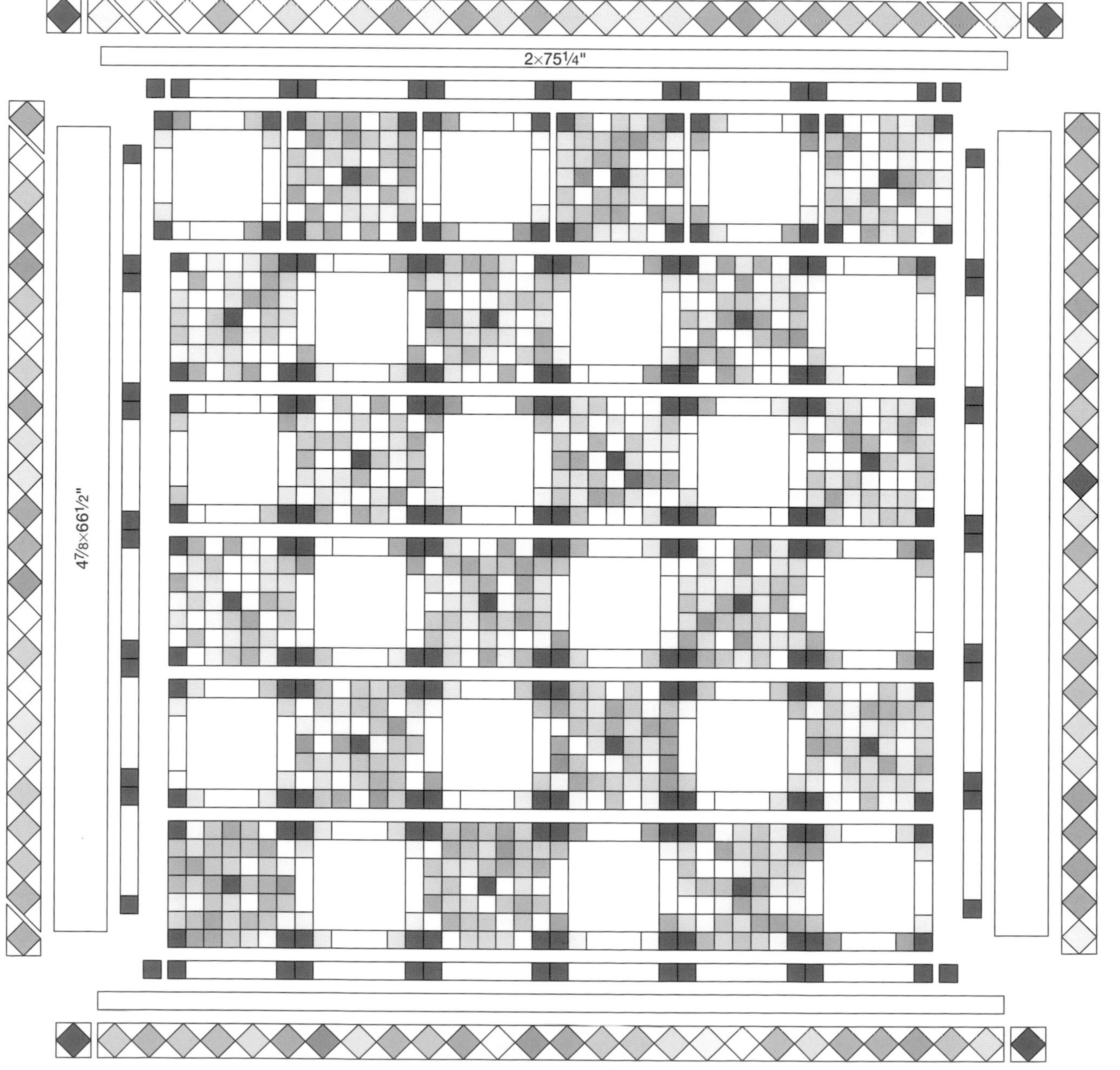

Quilt Assembly Diagram

strip. Press seams in one direction. The long outer border strip should be 3⅜×81" including seam allowances. Repeat to make a second long outer border strip.

6. Sew short outer border strips to short edges of quilt center. Sew long outer border strips to remaining edges to complete quilt top. Press all seams toward middle border.

Finish Quilt

1. Layer quilt top, batting, and backing; baste. (For details, see Complete Quilt, *page 159*.)

2. Quilt as desired. A 1"-wide diagonal grid is hand-quilted through the blocks on this antique quilt, and a cable design is stitched in the middle border.

3. Bind with solid blue binding strips. (For details, see Complete Quilt.)

RED ZINGER THROW

A splash of red punctuates a vast array of black-and-white prints.

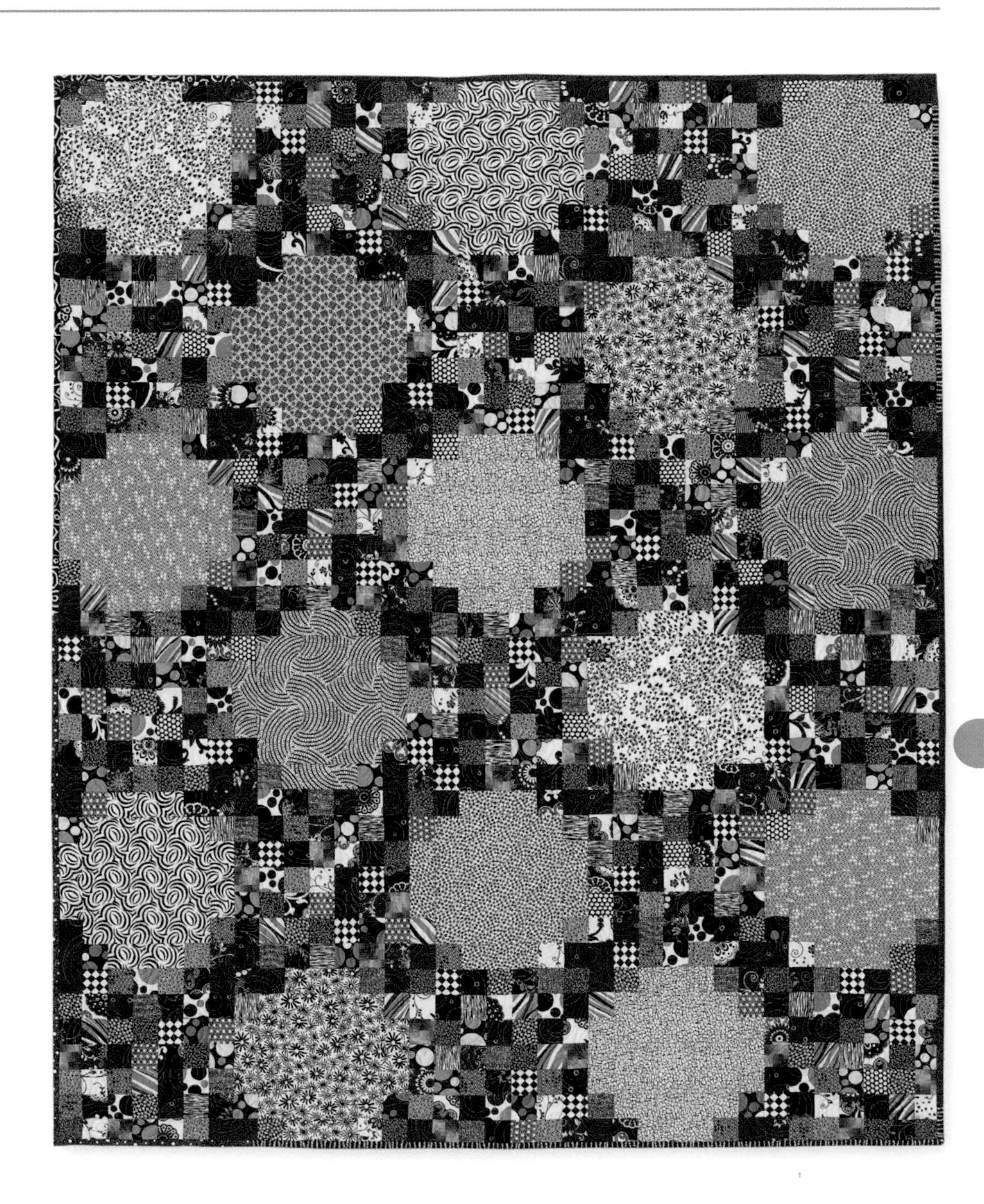

Materials

2¼ yards total assorted black-and-white prints (blocks)

15—9×22" pieces (fat eighths) assorted white prints (blocks)

⅔ yard total assorted red prints (blocks)

½ yard total assorted black prints (binding)

3½ yards backing fabric

61×72" batting

Finished quilt: 53×63½"

Cut Fabrics

Cut pieces in the following order.

The featured quilt showcases assorted red prints randomly placed among black-and-white prints. Follow the cutting instructions on *page 32* and the photo, *right,* to achieve the look of this quilt.

continued

From assorted black-and-white prints, cut:
- 748—2" squares

From *each* assorted white print, cut:
- 1—8" square
- 4—2×5" rectangles

From assorted red prints, cut:
- 167—2" squares

From assorted black prints, cut:
- 6—2½×42" binding strips

Assemble A Blocks

1. Gather one 8" square and four 2×5" rectangles from the same white print, eight assorted black-and-white print 2" squares, and four assorted red print 2" squares.

2. Referring to Assemble A Blocks, Step 1, *page 27,* sew assorted black-and-white print 2" squares to opposite ends of a white print 2×5" rectangle to make a small pieced rectangle. Repeat to make four small pieced rectangles total.

3. Referring to Assemble A Blocks, Step 2, *page 27,* sew assorted red print 2" squares to opposite ends of a small pieced rectangle to make a large pieced rectangle. Repeat to make a second large pieced rectangle.

4. Referring to Assemble A Blocks, steps 3 and 4, *page 28,* use small pieced rectangles, a white print 8" square, and large pieced rectangles to make an A block **(Diagram 11).**

5. Repeat steps 1–4 to make 15 A blocks total.

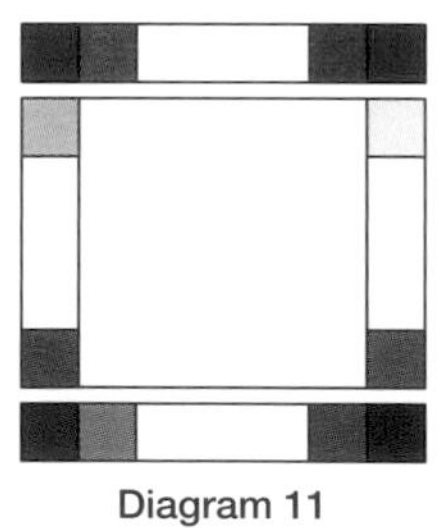
Diagram 11

Assemble B Blocks

1. Referring to **Diagram 12,** lay out four assorted red print 2" squares (one in each corner) and a total of 45 assorted black-and-white print and assorted red print 2" squares in seven horizontal rows (the number and placement of red print squares in each B block of the featured quilt varies; see photo *page 31*).

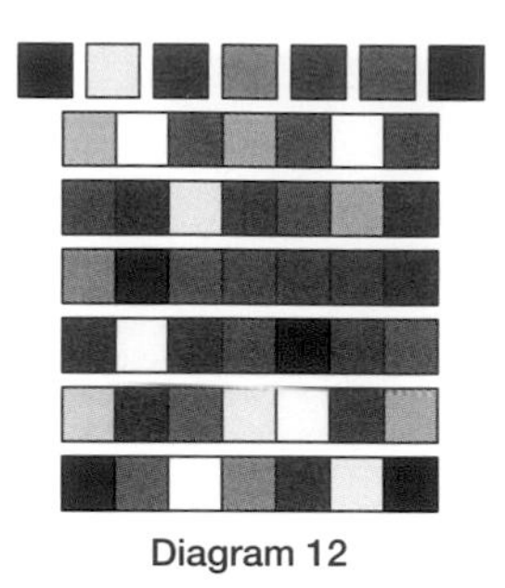
Diagram 12

2. Referring to Assemble B Blocks, steps 2 and 3, *page 29,* sew together squares to make a B Block.

3. Repeat steps 1 and 2 to make 15 B blocks total.

Assemble Quilt Top

1. Referring to photo, *page 31,* lay out blocks in six rows, alternating A and B blocks.

2. Sew together blocks in each row; press seams in one direction, alternating direction with each row. Join rows to complete quilt top. Press seams in one direction.

Finish Quilt

1. Layer quilt top, batting, and backing; baste. (For details, see Complete Quilt, *page 159.*)

2. Quilt as desired. Swirls and curlicues are machine-quilted across the featured quilt top.

3. Using straight seams, sew together assorted black print binding strips to make a pieced binding strip. Bind quilt with pieced binding strip. (For details, see Complete Quilt.)

FLORAL WALL QUILT

Showcase a large floral in the setting squares and a complementary small print in the quick-piece strip sets for a stunning wall quilt.

Materials

- 5/8 yard purple print (blocks, binding)
- 3/8 yard green print (blocks)
- 18×22" piece (fat quarter) yellow print (blocks)
- 9×22" piece (fat eighth) cream print (blocks)
- 2/3 yard purple floral (setting squares)
- 1 1/8 yards backing fabric
- 40" square batting

Finished quilt: 32" square

Cut Fabrics

Cut pieces in the following order.

From purple print, cut:
- 4—2½×42" binding strips
- 7—2×21" strips

From green print, cut:
- 11—2×21" strips

From yellow print, cut:
- 7—2×21" strips

From cream print, cut:
- 3—2×21" strips

From purple floral, cut:
- 4—11" setting squares

Assemble Blocks

1. Referring to **Diagram 13,** sew together two purple print 2×21" strips, two green print 2×21" strips, two yellow print 2×21" strips, and one cream print 2×21" strip to make strip set A. Press seams in direction indicated by arrow in **Diagram 13.** Cut strip set into 10—2"-wide A segments.

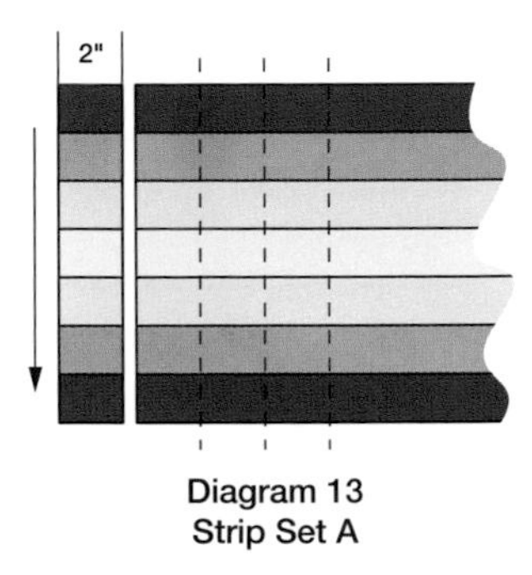

Diagram 13
Strip Set A

2. Join four green print 2×21" strips, two purple print 2×21" strips, and one yellow print 2×21" strip to make strip set B **(Diagram 14)**; press seams in direction indicated by arrow. Cut strip set into 10—2"-wide B segments.

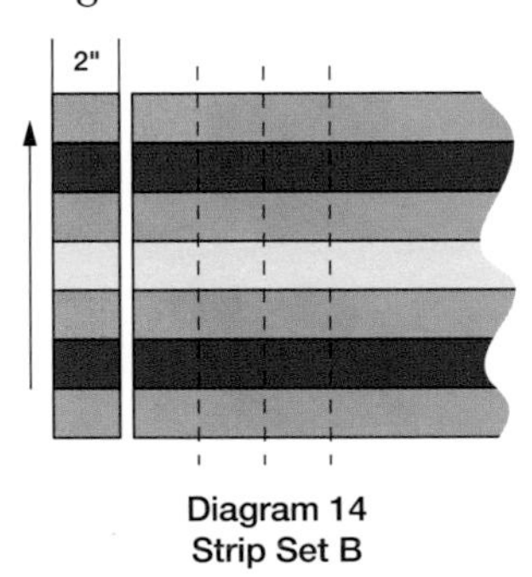

Diagram 14
Strip Set B

3. Sew together two yellow print 2×21" strips, three green print 2×21" strips, and two purple print 2×21" strips to make strip set C **(Diagram 15)**; press seams in direction indicated by arrow. Cut strip set into 10—2"-wide C segments.

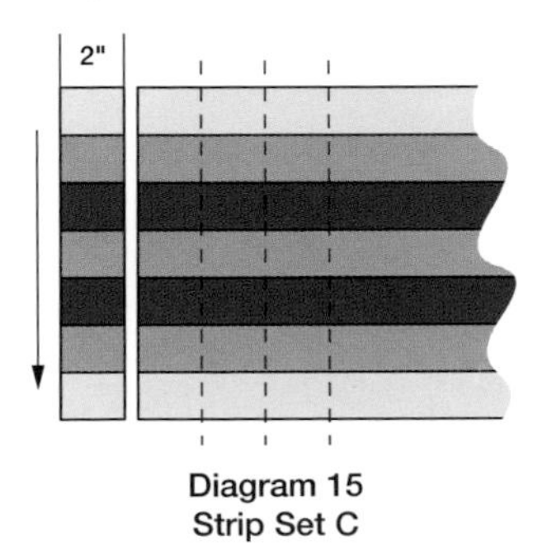

Diagram 15
Strip Set C

4. Join two cream print 2×21" strips, two yellow print 2×21" strips, two green print 2×21" strips, and one purple print 2×21" strip to make strip set D **(Diagram 16)**; press seams in direction indicated by arrow. Cut strip set into five 2"-wide D segments.

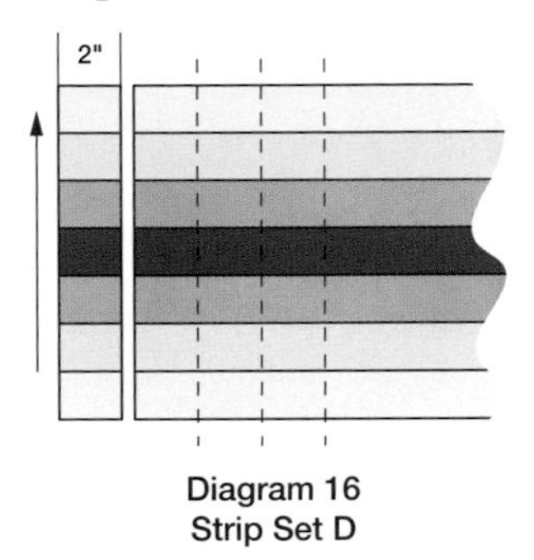

Diagram 16
Strip Set D

5. Referring to **Diagram 17**, lay out two *each* of segments A, B, and C and one segment D in seven vertical rows. Join rows to make a block. Press seams in one direction. The block should be 11" square including seam allowances. Repeat to make five blocks total.

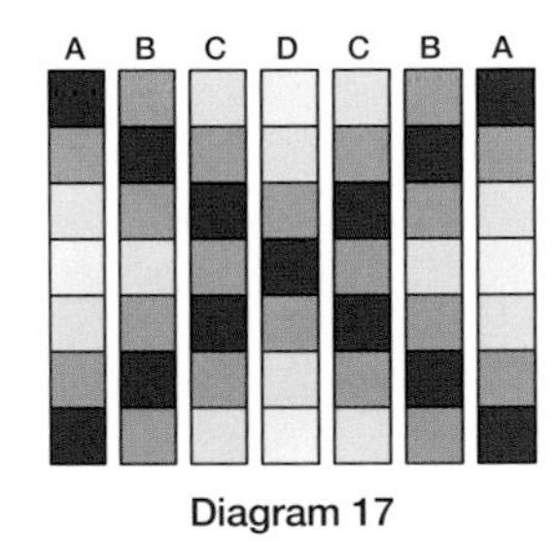

Diagram 17

Assemble Quilt Top

1. Referring to photo, *opposite,* lay out blocks and purple floral setting squares in three rows.

2. Sew together pieces in each row; press seams toward purple floral squares. Join rows to complete quilt top. Press seams in one direction.

Finish Quilt

1. Layer quilt top, batting, and backing; baste. (For details, see Complete Quilt, *page 159.*)

2. Quilt as desired. Using variegated thread, a feathered wreath is machine-quilted in each block, and a grid is stitched through each setting square.

3. Bind with purple print binding strips. (For details, see Complete Quilt.)

38
66
55
48

ROTARY-CUT CHARMERS

Utilizing a rotary cutter, mat, and acrylic ruler makes fast work of cutting accurate fabric pieces. There are many choices of rotary-cutting tools available at quilt shops and fabric stores, and what you select depends on your task and preferences. Cutting numerous strips and squares for the projects in this chapter will give you an opportunity to perfect your rotary-cutting skills.

CABIN *Cozy*

Be ready for cool days ahead with Kim Diehl's delightfully scrappy throw. Kim chose Bear's Paw units as the focal point of Log Cabin blocks and border corners.

Materials

1¼ yards total assorted medium to dark prints in red, blue, gold, green, and purple (blocks, inner and outer borders, binding)

1½ yards total assorted tan prints (blocks, sashing)

1½ yards total assorted cream prints (blocks, sashing)

1⅓ yards cranberry print (sashing; inner, middle, and outer borders)

18×22" piece (fat quarter) ivory print (inner and outer borders)

⅓ yard gold print (middle and outer borders)

3⅔ yards backing fabric

66" square batting

Finished quilt: 57½" square
Finished blocks: 6" square

Quantities are for 44/45"-wide, 100% cotton fabrics. **Measurements** include ¼" seam allowances. Sew with right sides together unless otherwise stated.

Designer Notes

For this scrap quilt, designer Kim Diehl pulled more than 50 different fabrics from her stash. Although the design appears random, Kim put a great deal of planning into the fabric placement. For example, she alternated cream prints with tan prints in the horizontal sashing strips. In addition, she alternated contrasting vertical sashing strips so that the tan strips butt up against the Bear's Paw units.

Cut Fabrics

Cut pieces in the following order. Cut cranberry print border strips lengthwise (parallel to the selvages).

From assorted medium to dark prints, cut:

- Enough 2½"-wide strips in lengths ranging from 12" to 32" to total 250" in length for binding
- 52—2½" squares
- 104—1⅞" squares, cutting each in half diagonally for 208 triangles total

From assorted tan prints, cut:

- 62—1½×6½" strips for blocks and sashing
- 36—1½×5½" strips
- 36—1½×4½" strips
- 18—1½×3½" strips
- 36—1⅞" squares, cutting each in half diagonally for 72 triangles total
- 18—1½" squares

continued

From assorted cream prints, cut:

- 58—1½×6½" strips for blocks and sashing
- 36—1½×5½" strips
- 36—1½×4½" strips
- 18—1½×3½" strips
- 36—1⅞" squares, cutting each in half diagonally for 72 triangles total
- 18—1½" squares

From cranberry print, cut:

- 8—3½×43½" strips for inner and outer borders
- 53—1½" squares for sashing and middle border

From ivory print, cut:

- 32—1⅞" squares, cutting each in half diagonally for 64 triangles total
- 16—1½" squares

From gold print, cut:

- 5—1½×42" strips for middle border
- 8—1½×3½" rectangles for outer border

Assemble Bear's Paw Units

1. Sew together an assorted medium or dark print triangle and an assorted tan print triangle to make a tan triangle-square **(Diagram 1).** Press seam toward medium or dark print triangle. The triangle-square should be 1½" square including seam allowances. Repeat to make 72 tan triangle-squares total.

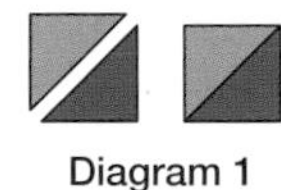
Diagram 1

2. Using assorted medium or dark print triangles and assorted cream print triangles, repeat Step 1 to make 72 cream triangle-squares total.

3. Referring to **Diagram 2**, lay out two tan triangle-squares, two cream triangle-squares, one assorted medium or dark print 2½" square, and one assorted tan print 1½" square in sections. Join the two cream triangle-squares; press seam in one direction. Then sew together pieces in each horizontal row; press seams in opposite directions. Join sections to make a Bear's Paw unit A; press seam in one direction. The unit should be 3½" square including seam allowances. Repeat to make 18 Bear's Paw A units total.

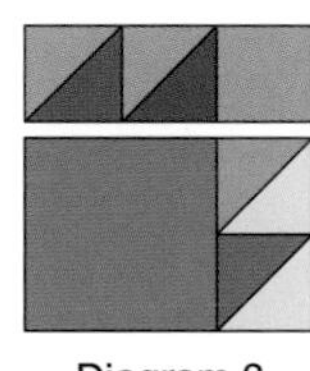
Diagram 2
Unit A

4. Using two cream triangle-squares, two tan triangle-squares, one assorted medium or dark print 2½" square, and one assorted cream print 1½" square, repeat Step 3 to make 18 Bear's Paw B units **(Diagram 3).**

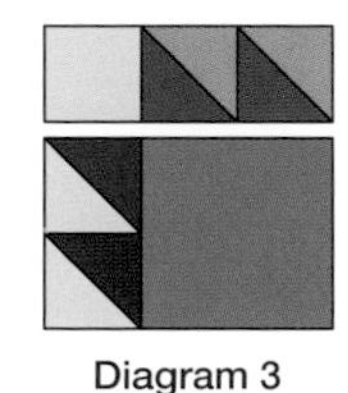
Diagram 3
Unit B

Assemble Blocks

1. Referring to **Diagram 4**, sew together a Bear's Paw unit A and an assorted cream print 1½×3½" strip. Press seam toward cream print strip.

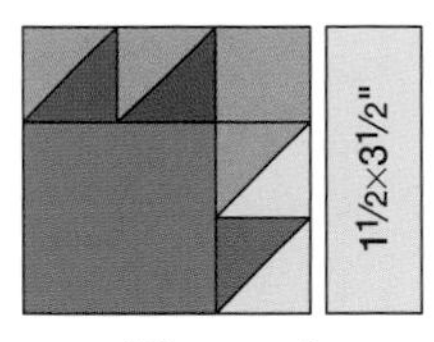

Diagram 4

2. Referring to **Diagram 5**, add an assorted tan print 1½×4½" strip to adjacent edge of Bear's Paw unit. Continue adding strips, alternating assorted cream and tan prints in same manner, to make block A. Press all seams away from Bear's Paw unit A. The block should be 6½" square including seam allowances.

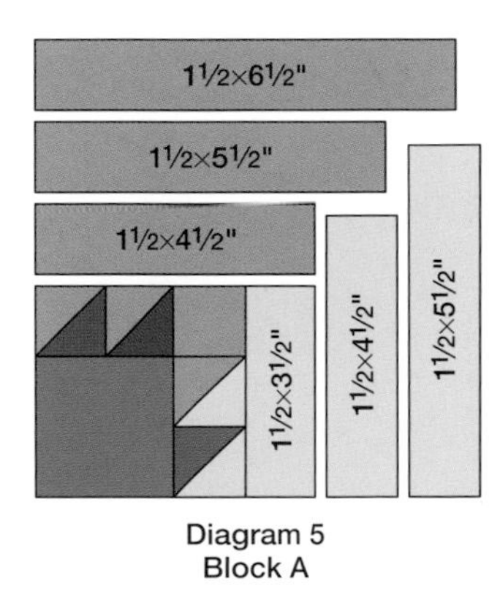

Diagram 5
Block A

3. Repeat steps 1 and 2 to make 18 A blocks total.

4. Referring to **Diagram 6**, sew together a Bear's Paw unit B and an assorted tan print 1½×3½" strip. Add remaining strips as shown in diagram to make block B. Press all seams away from Bear's Paw unit B. The block should be 6½" square including seam allowances. Repeat to make 18 B blocks total.

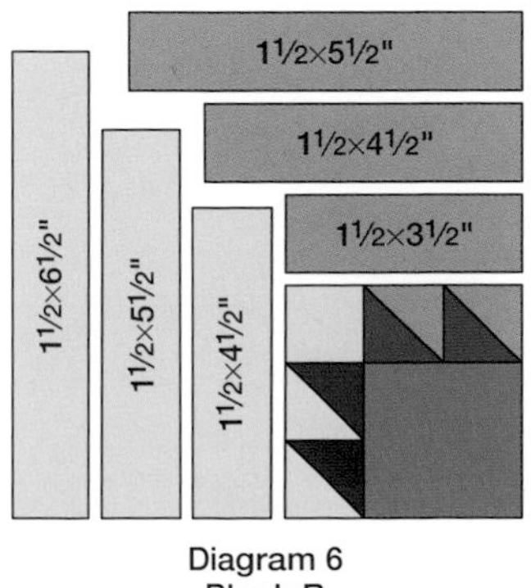

Diagram 6
Block B

continued

Assemble Quilt Center

1. Referring to **Quilt Assembly Diagram**, lay out A and B blocks, 40 assorted cream print and 44 assorted tan print 1½×6½" sashing strips, and 49 cranberry print 1½" sashing squares in 13 horizontal rows.

2. Sew together pieces in each row; press seams toward sashing strips. Join rows to make quilt center; press seams in one direction. The quilt center should be 43½" square including seam allowances.

Assemble and Add Borders

1. Referring to Assemble Bear's Paw Units, Step 1, *page 41,* use assorted medium and dark print triangles and ivory print triangles to make 64 ivory triangle-squares.

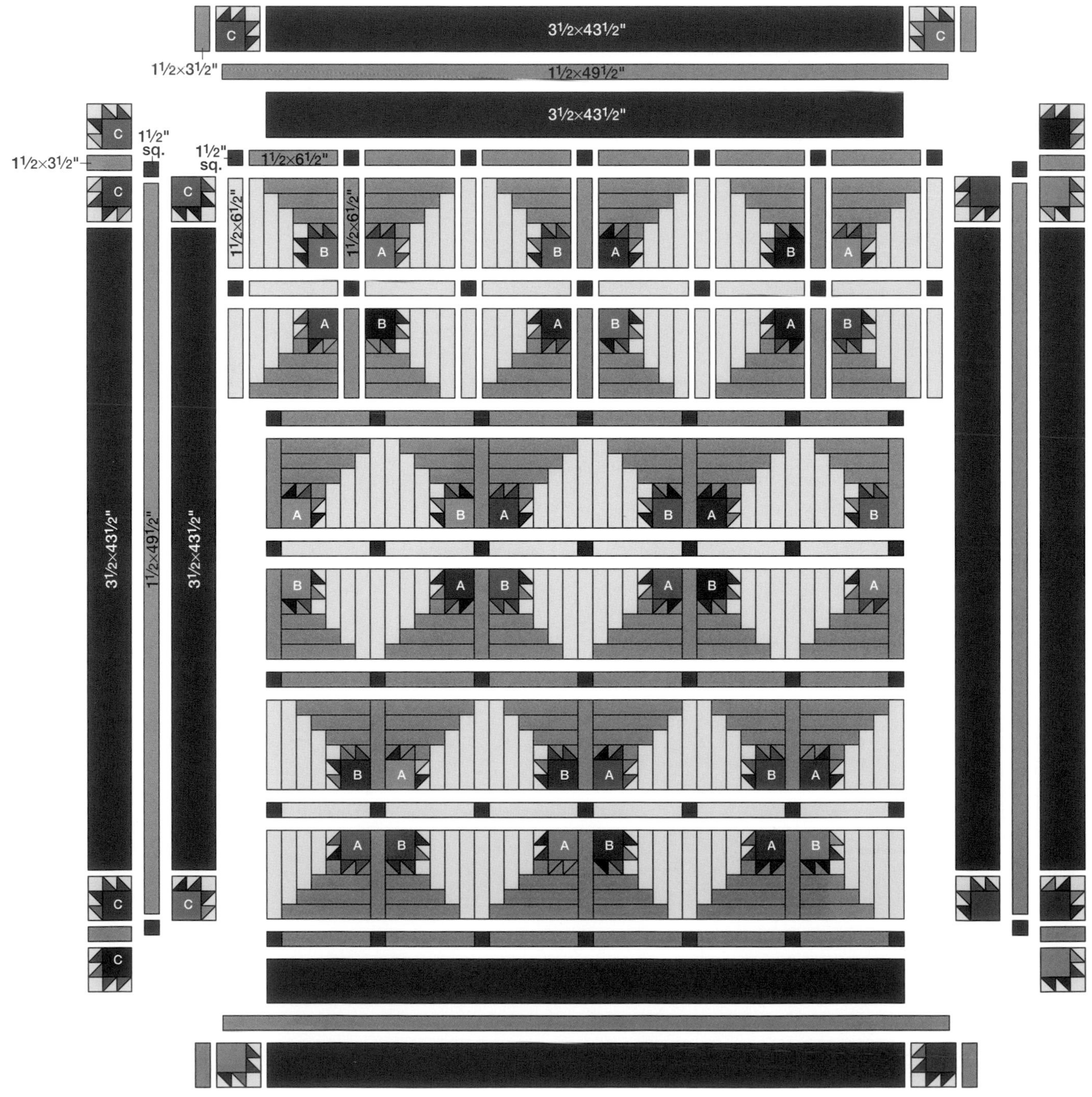

Quilt Assembly Diagram

2. Referring to **Diagram 7** and Assemble Bear's Paw Units, Step 3, *page 41,* use four ivory triangle-squares, one assorted medium or dark print 2½" square, and one ivory print 1½" square to make a Bear's Paw unit C. Repeat to make 16 Bear's Paw C units total.

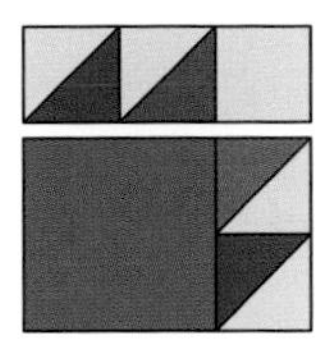

Diagram 7

3. Sew cranberry print border strips to opposite edges of quilt center. Press seams toward border.

4. Referring to **Quilt Assembly Diagram**, sew a Bear's Paw unit C to each end of a remaining cranberry print border strip to make a long inner border strip. Press seams toward cranberry print strip. Repeat to make a second long inner border strip. Sew long inner border strips to remaining edges of quilt center. Press seams toward border.

5. Cut and piece gold print 1½×42" strips to make:
4—1½×49½" middle border strips

6. Sew middle border strips to opposite edges of quilt center. Press seams toward middle border.

7. Sew a cranberry print 1½" square to each end of a remaining middle border strip to make a long middle border strip. Press seams toward gold print. Repeat to make a second long middle border strip. Sew long middle border strips to remaining edges of quilt center. Press seams toward middle border.

8. Sew a Bear's Paw unit C and a gold print 1½×3½" rectangle to each end of a remaining cranberry print border strip to make a short outer border strip (**Quilt Assembly Diagram;** note placement of Bear's Paw units). Press seams away from Bear's Paw units. Repeat to make four short outer border strips total.

9. Sew short outer border strips to opposite edges of quilt center. Press seams toward outer border.

10. Sew a Bear's Paw unit C to each end of a remaining short outer border strip to make a long outer border strip. Press seams away from Bear's Paw units. Repeat to make a second long outer border strip. Sew long outer border strips to remaining edges to complete quilt top. Press seams toward middle border.

Finish Quilt

1. Layer quilt top, batting, and backing; baste. (For details, see Complete Quilt, *page 159.*) Quilt as desired.

2. Using straight seams, sew together assorted medium and dark print 2½"-wide strips to make a pieced binding strip. Bind quilt with pieced binding strip. (For details, see Complete Quilt.)

optional colors

Autumn Glow

Assorted prints from her fabric stash prompted quilt tester Laura Boehnke to make a table runner echoing autumn's final burst of color. The same print is used for the Bear's Paw units and the sashing squares to create contrast and continuity. Laura also carefully chose prints for the vertical sashing strips that repeat the colors of the adjacent blocks.

BLUE-AND-WHITE LOG CABINS

A classic pattern and tried-and-true color combo always look great together.

Materials

$\frac{1}{4}$ yard white floral No. 1 (blocks)

$\frac{1}{2}$ yard light blue floral (blocks)

$\frac{1}{3}$ yard *each* of dark blue floral No. 1 and white floral No. 2 (blocks)

$\frac{3}{8}$ yard *each* of dark blue floral No. 2 and white floral No. 3 (blocks)

$\frac{1}{2}$ yard dark blue floral No. 3 (blocks)

$\frac{3}{8}$ yard dark blue tone-on-tone (binding)

1$\frac{1}{4}$ yards backing fabric

45" square batting

Finished quilt: 36½" square

Cut Fabrics

Cut pieces in the following order.

From white floral No. 1, cut:
- 36—1½×3½" strips

From light blue floral, cut:
- 36—3½" squares

From *each* of dark blue floral No. 1 and white floral No. 2, cut:
- 36—1½×4½" strips

From *each* of dark blue floral No. 2 and white floral No. 3, cut:
- 36—1½×5½" strips

From dark blue floral No. 3, cut:
- 36—1½×6½" strips

From dark blue tone-on-tone, cut:
- 4—2½×42½" binding strips

Assemble Blocks

1. Referring to **Diagram 8**, sew a white floral No. 1—1½×3½" strip to one edge of a light blue floral 3½" square. Press seam toward white floral strip.

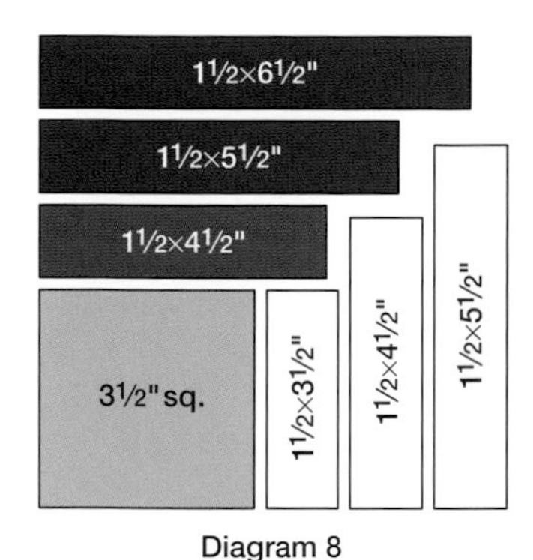

Diagram 8

2. Add a dark blue floral No. 1—1½×4½" strip to top adjacent edge of light blue floral 3½" square. Continue adding strips, alternating white floral and dark blue floral strips in same manner, to make a block **(Diagram 8).** Press all seams away from light blue floral 3½" square. The block should be 6½" square including seam allowances.

3. Repeat steps 1 and 2 to make 36 blocks total.

Assemble Quilt Top

1. Referring to **Quilt Assembly Diagram**, lay out blocks in six horizontal rows, rotating blocks as shown.

2. Sew together pieces in each row; press seams in one direction, alternating direction with each row. Join rows to complete quilt top; press seams in one direction.

Finish Quilt

1. Layer quilt top, batting, and backing; baste. (For details, see Complete Quilt, *page 159*.)

2. Quilt as desired. This project features allover loops and curlicues.

3. Bind with dark blue tone-on-tone binding strips. (For details, see Complete Quilt.)

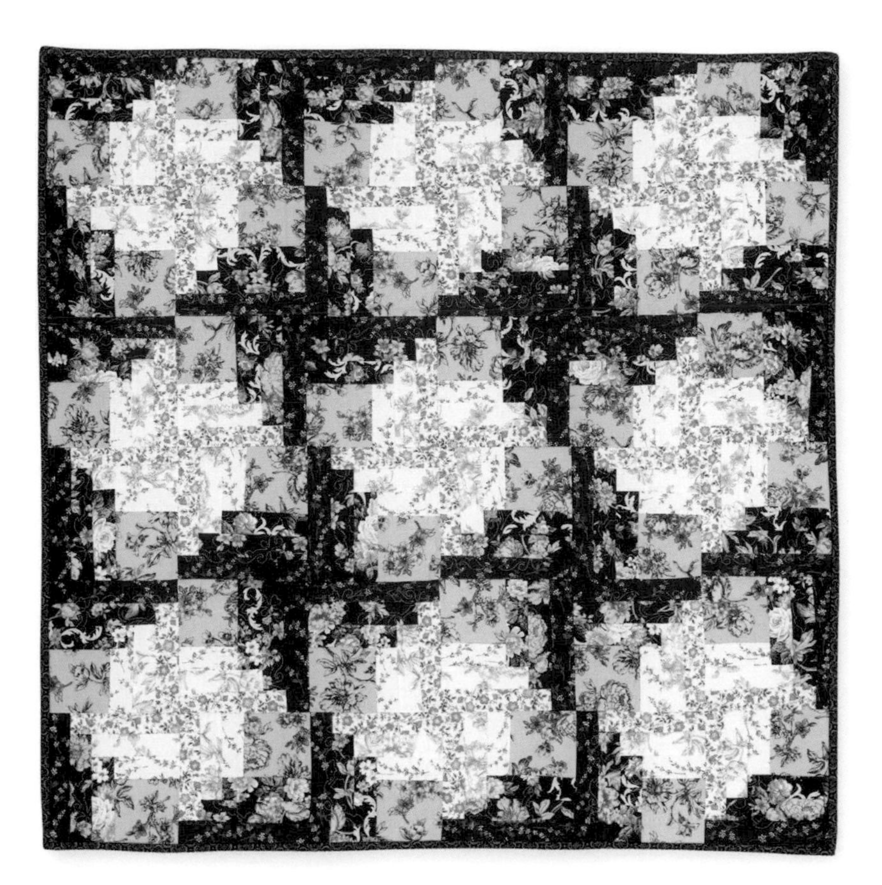

Quilt Assembly Diagram

BEAR'S PAW MESSAGE BOARD

Surround four Bear's Paw blocks with bright, cheery prints.

Materials

9×22" piece (fat eighth) pink tone-on-tone (blocks)
9×22" piece (fat eighth) blue-and-green dot (blocks)
Scraps of assorted prints, plaids, and dots in green, blue, and pink (quilt center)
1/4 yard green floral (border)
12" square craft felt
12" square corkboard
Stapler
Craft glue
Picture hanger (optional)

Finished message board: 12" square
Finished block: 3" square

Cut Fabrics

Cut pieces in the following order.

From pink tone-on-tone, cut:

- 4—2½" squares
- 8—1⅞" squares, cutting each in half diagonally for 16 triangles total

From blue-and-green dot, cut:

- 8—1⅞" squares, cutting each in half diagonally for 16 triangles total
- 4—1½" squares

From assorted prints, plaids, and dots, cut:

- 12—3½" squares

From green floral, cut:

- 2—2½×16½" border strips
- 2—2½×12½" border strips

Assemble Bear's Paw Blocks

1. Referring to Assemble Bear's Paw Units, Step 1, *page 41,* use pink tone-on-tone triangles and blue-and-green dot triangles to make 16 triangle-squares.

2. Referring to **Diagram 9**, and Assemble Bear's Paw Units, Step 3, *page 41*, use four triangle-squares, one pink tone-on-tone 2½" square, and one blue-and-green dot 1½" square to make a Bear's Paw block. Repeat to make four Bear's Paw blocks total.

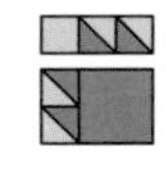

Diagram 9

Assemble Quilt Top

1. Referring to **Diagram 10**, lay out assorted print, plaid, and dot 3½" squares and Bear's Paw blocks in four rows.

2. Sew together pieces in each row; press seams in one direction, alternating direction with each row. Join rows to make quilt center; press seams in one direction. The quilt center should be 12½" square including seam allowances.

3. Sew green floral 2½×12½" border strips to opposite edges of quilt center. Add green floral 2½×16½" border strips to remaining edges to complete quilt top. Press all seams toward border.

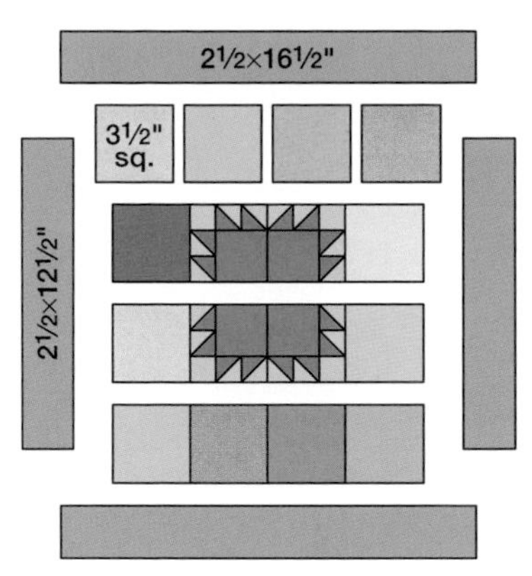

Diagram 10

Finish Message Board

1. Lay quilt top, wrong side up, on table. Center corkboard over quilt top.

2. Pull one border to back of corkboard, making sure fabric is taut. Using an opened office stapler, secure border with a row of staples about 1" from edge of corkboard, spacing staples about 1" apart **(Diagram 11).**

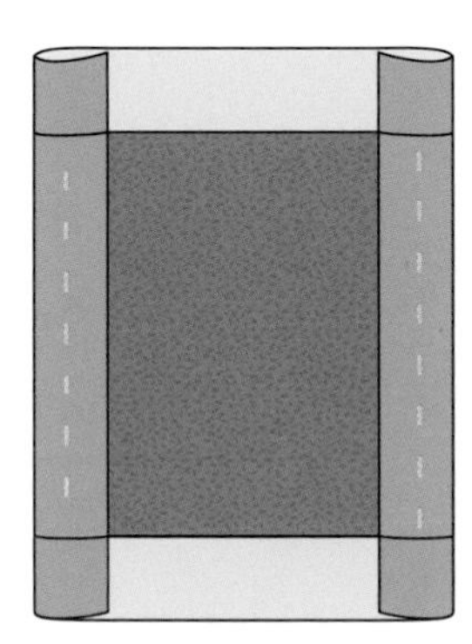

Diagram 11

3. Repeat Step 2 on opposite border. Continue with remaining borders, folding in corners neatly.

4. Glue 12" square of craft felt to back of corkboard to cover raw edges and complete message board. Add hanger, if desired.

WALLED *Garden*

Designer Sheila Sinclair Snyder's scrappy double-bed-size quilt is a great way to use up your fabric stash.

Materials

30—18×22" pieces (fat quarters) assorted pink prints (blocks)

4⅞ yards total assorted green, brown, and burgundy prints (blocks, binding)

7½ yards backing fabric

89×105" batting

Finished quilt: 80½×96½"
Finished blocks: 8" square

Quantities are for 44/45"-wide, 100% cotton fabrics. **Measurements** include ¼" seam allowances. Sew with right sides together unless otherwise stated.

SIZE OPTIONS: For a chart of optional sizes, turn to *Pattern Sheet 2.*

Designer Notes

Designer Sheila Sinclair Snyder chose a wide variety of light to medium pink prints—more than 30 in all—for the quilt's background. Using about 30 contrasting greens, browns, and burgundies in medium to dark hues allowed the design to emerge.

Sheila focuses many of her quilt designs on building the borders as block units, rather than in long strips.

"This keeps the measurements small and manageable and the pieces easier to work with," she says. "Since the borders are set as blocks that are the same size as the blocks within the quilt, they fit together perfectly smooth and flat."

Cut Fabrics

Cut pieces in the order that follows in each section.

Cut and Assemble Double Four-Patch Blocks

The following instructions result in two identical Double Four-Patch blocks. Repeat cutting and assembly steps to make 80 Double Four-Patch blocks total.

From one assorted pink print, cut:

- 1—2½×21" strip
- 4—4½" squares

From one assorted green, brown, or burgundy print, cut:

- 1—2½×21" strip

continued

1. Aligning long edges, sew together pink print 2½×21" strip and green, brown, or burgundy print 2½×21" strip to make a strip set **(Diagram 1)**. Press seam toward green, brown, or burgundy print strip. Cut strip set into eight 2½"-wide segments.

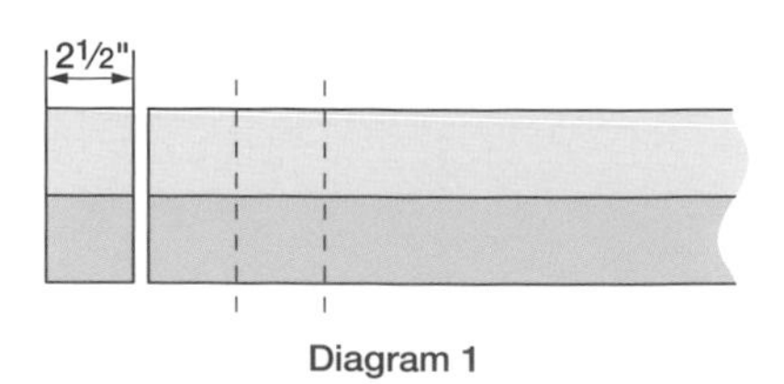

Diagram 1

2. Sew together two 2½"-wide segments to make a Four-Patch unit **(Diagram 2)**. Press seam in one direction. The Four-Patch unit should be 4½" square including seam allowances. Repeat to make four Four-Patch units total.

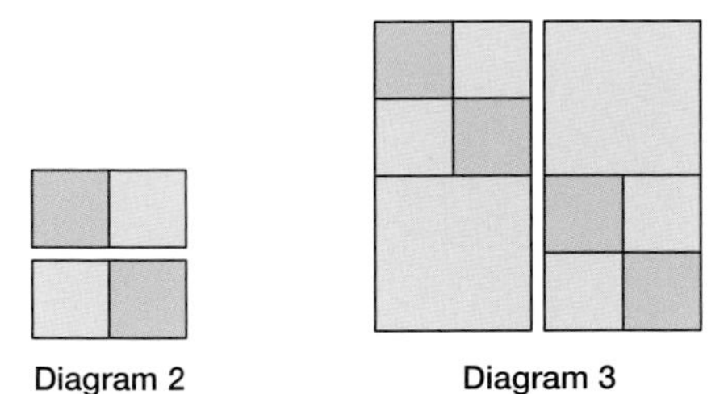
Diagram 2 Diagram 3

3. Referring to **Diagram 3**, sew together two Four-Patch units and two pink print 4½" squares in pairs. Press seams toward pink print squares. Join pairs to make a Double Four-Patch block; press seam in one direction. The block should be 8½" square including seam allowances. Repeat to make a matching Double Four-Patch block.

Cut and Assemble Four-Patch Triangles

The following instructions result in one Four-Patch triangle. Repeat cutting and assembly steps to make 40 Four-Patch triangles total.

From one assorted pink print, cut:
- 1—4⅞" square, cutting it in half diagonally for 2 triangles total
- 2—2½" squares

From one assorted green, brown, or burgundy print, cut:
- 2—2½" squares

1. Referring to **Diagram 2**, sew together pink print 2½" squares and green, brown, or burgundy print 2½" squares in pairs. Press seams toward green, brown, or burgundy print squares. Join pairs to make a Four-Patch unit; press seam in one direction. The Four-Patch unit should be 4½" square including seam allowances.

2. Referring to **Diagram 4**, sew pink print triangles to adjacent edges of Four-Patch unit to make a Four-Patch triangle. Press seams toward pink print triangles.

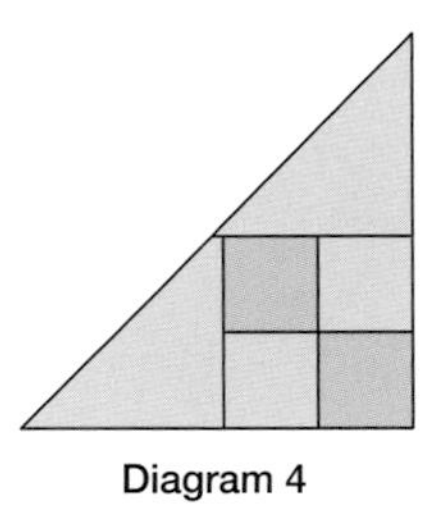
Diagram 4

Cut and Assemble Roman Stripe Triangles

The Triangle Template is on *Pattern Sheet 1*. To make a template of the pattern, see Make and Use Templates, *page 157*.

From assorted green, brown, and burgundy prints, cut:
- 48—1½×42" strips

1. Aligning long edges, sew together six assorted green, brown, and burgundy print 1½×42" strips to make a strip set. Press seams in one direction. Repeat to make eight strip sets total.

2. Referring to **Diagram 5**, use triangle template to cut five triangles per strip set to make 40 Roman Stripe triangles total. By rotating the template each time you cut a triangle, you'll create more variety in the resulting Roman Stripe triangles.

Assemble Modified Roman Stripe Blocks

Sew together a Four-Patch triangle and a Roman Stripe triangle to make a modified Roman Stripe block **(Diagram 6)**. Press seam toward Roman Stripe triangle. The block should be 8½" square including seam allowances. Repeat to make 40 modified Roman Stripe blocks total.

continued

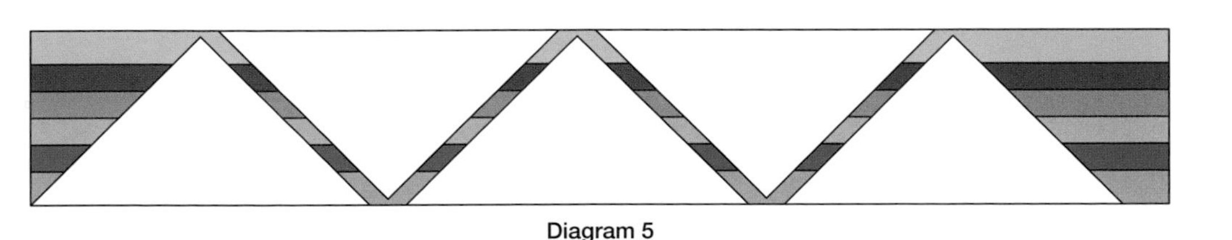
Diagram 5

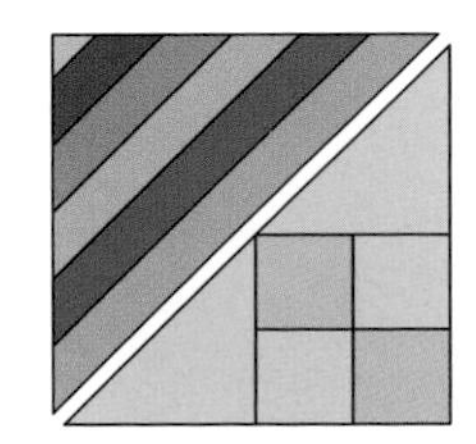
Diagram 6

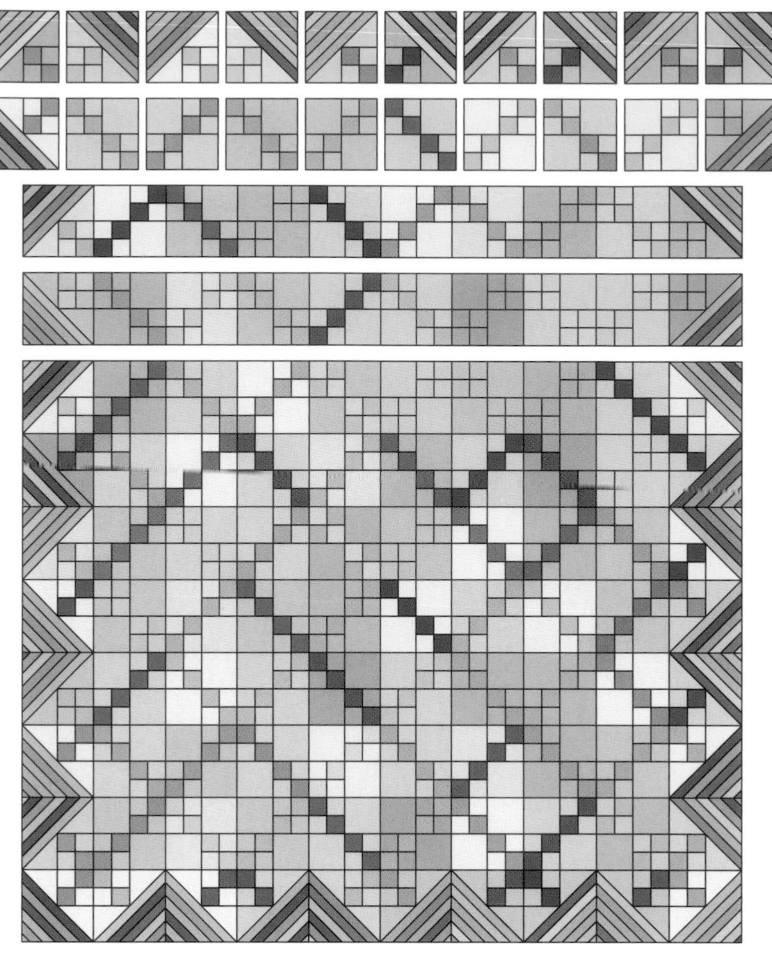
Quilt Assembly Diagram

Assemble Quilt Top

1. Referring to **Quilt Assembly Diagram**, lay out Double Four-Patch blocks and modified Roman Stripe blocks in 12 horizontal rows.

2. Sew together blocks in each row. Press seams in one direction, alternating direction with each row. Join rows to complete quilt top. Press seams in one direction.

Finish Quilt

From assorted green, brown, and burgundy prints, cut: 20—2½×21" binding strips.

1. Layer quilt top, batting, and backing; baste. (For details, see Complete Quilt, *page 159*.)

2. Quilt as desired. Sheila machine-quilted this bed quilt in an allover ribbon design.

3. Using diagonal seams, join assorted green, brown, and burgundy print 2½×21"-wide strips to make a pieced binding strip. Bind quilt with pieced binding strip. (For details, see Complete Quilt.)

TRANQUIL BREEZES QUILT

A soothing sea glass and sand color palette lends an air of serenity to a Double Four-Patch quilt.

Materials

2⅞ yards mottled aqua (blocks, binding)

5¾ yards mottled cream (blocks)

7½ yards backing fabric

89×105" batting

Finished quilt: 80½×96½"

Cut Fabrics

Cut pieces in the following order.

From mottled aqua, cut:
- 39—2½×42" strips for blocks and binding

From mottled cream, cut:
- 30—2½×42" strips
- 240—4½" squares

1. Referring to **Diagram 1**, *page 50*, sew together a mottled aqua 2½×42" strip and a mottled cream 2½×42" strip to make a strip set. Press seam toward mottled aqua strip. Repeat to make 30 strip sets total. Cut strip sets into 480—2½"-wide segments total.

2. Referring to Cut and Assemble Double Four-Patch Blocks, Step 2, *page 51*, use 2½"-wide segments to make 240 Four-Patch units.

3. Referring to Cut and Assemble Double Four-Patch Blocks, Step 3, *page 51*, use Four-Patch units and mottled cream 4½" squares to make 120 Double Four-Patch blocks.

Assemble Quilt Top

1. Referring to photo on *page 54*, lay out Double Four-Patch blocks in 12 horizontal rows.

continued

2. Sew together blocks in each row. Press seams in one direction, alternating direction with each row. Join rows to complete quilt top. Press seams in one direction.

Finish Quilt

1. Layer quilt top, batting, and backing; baste. (For details, see Complete Quilt, *page 159*.)

2. Quilt as desired. The featured quilt is stitched in an allover swirl pattern.

3. Bind with remaining mottled aqua 2½×42" strips. (For details, see Complete Quilt.)

BOUNTIFUL HARVEST THROW

A blend of fabrics in autumn's vibrant hues results in a charming scrappy throw.

Materials

5/8 yard multicolor paisley (binding)

2⅔ yards total assorted light prints (blocks)

3⅜ yards total assorted medium and dark prints (blocks)

4⅛ yards backing fabric

73" square batting

continued

Finished quilt: 64½" square

Cut Fabrics

Cut pieces in the order that follows in each section.

From multicolor paisley, cut:
- 7—2½×42" binding strips

Cut and Assemble Double Four-Patch Blocks

The following instructions result in one Double Four-Patch block. Repeat cutting and assembly steps to make 16 Double Four-Patch blocks total.

From one assorted light print, cut:
- 1—2½×11" strip
- 2—4½" squares

From one assorted medium or dark print, cut:
- 1—2½×11" strip

Quilt Assembly Diagram

1. Referring to Cut and Assemble Double Four-Patch Blocks, Step 1, *page 50,* use light print 2½×11" strip and medium or dark print 2½×11" strip to make a strip set. Cut strip set into four 2½"-wide segments.

2. Referring to Cut and Assemble Double Four-Patch Blocks, Step 2, *page 51,* use 2½"-wide segments to make two Four-Patch units.

3. Referring to Cut and Assemble Double Four-Patch Blocks, Step 3, *page 51,* use Four-Patch units and light print 4½" squares to make a Double Four-Patch block.

Cut and Assemble Four-Patch Triangles

The following instructions result in one Four-Patch triangle. Repeat cutting and assembly steps to make 48 Four-Patch triangles total.

From one assorted light print, cut:
- 1—4⅞" square, cutting it in half diagonally for 2 triangles total
- 2—2½" squares

From one assorted medium or dark print, cut:
- 2—2½" squares

Referring to Cut and Assemble Four-Patch Triangles, steps 1 and 2, *page 51,* use light print 2½" squares, medium or dark print 2½" squares, and light print triangles to make a Four-Patch triangle.

Cut and Assemble Roman Stripe Triangles

This project uses *Walled Garden* Triangle Template on *Pattern Sheet 1.*

From assorted light, medium, and dark prints, cut:
- 60—1½×42" strips

1. Referring to Cut and Assemble Roman Stripe Triangles, Step 1, *page 51,* use assorted print 1½×42" strips to make 10 strip sets total.

2. Referring to **Diagram 5** on *page 51,* use triangle template to cut five triangles per strip set to make 50 Roman Stripe triangles total (you will use 48).

Assemble Modified Roman Stripe Blocks

Referring to Assemble Modified Roman Stripe Blocks, *page 51,* use a Four-Patch triangle and a

Roman Stripe triangle to make a modified Roman Stripe block. Repeat to make 48 modified Roman Stripe blocks total.

Assemble Quilt Top

1. Referring to **Quilt Assembly Diagram**, *opposite,* lay out Double Four-Patch blocks and modified Roman Stripe blocks in eight horizontal rows.

2. Sew together blocks in each row. Press seams in one direction, alternating direction with each row. Join rows to complete quilt top. Press seams in one direction.

Finish Quilt

1. Layer quilt top, batting, and backing; baste. (For details, see Complete Quilt, *page 159.*)

2. Quilt as desired. The featured quilt is machine-quilted in a looping floral design.

3. Bind with multicolor paisley binding strips. (For details, see Complete Quilt.)

MIDNIGHT *Garden*

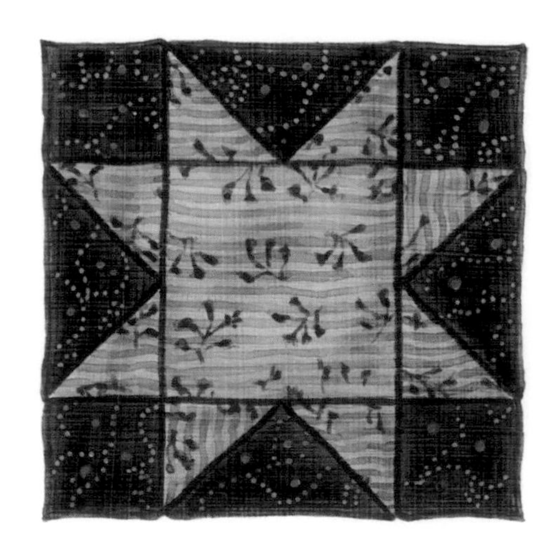

Evening Star blocks—light stars on dark backgrounds—provide the focal point on a toile wall hanging by designer Jo Morton.

Materials

18—6×8" rectangles assorted light prints in cream, tan, and gold (blocks)

5—8×15" pieces assorted black prints (blocks)

1½ yards black-and-gold stripe (blocks, sashing, inner border, binding)

(If you prefer single-fold binding, as designer Jo Morton does, you'll need 1⅓ yards.)

1½ yards black-and-tan toile (setting and corner triangles, outer border)

2½ yards backing fabric

43×56" batting

Finished quilt: 35×48"
Finished block: 4" square

Quantities are for 44/45"-wide, 100% cotton fabrics. **Measurements** include ¼" seam allowances. Sew with right sides together unless otherwise stated.

SIZE OPTIONS: For a chart of optional sizes, turn to *Pattern Sheet 2*.

Cut Fabrics

Cut pieces in the following order. Cut sashing, inner border, and outer border strips lengthwise (parallel to the selvages).

From *each* assorted light print, cut:
- 1—2½" square
- 4—1⅞" squares

From *each* assorted black print, cut:
- 3—3¼" squares
- 12—1½" squares

From black-and-gold stripe, cut:
- 5—2½×42" binding strips *or* 5—1⅛×42" strips for single-fold binding
- 2—2½×34½" sashing strips
- 2—1½×34½" inner border strips
- 2—1½×23½" inner border strips
- 3—3¼" squares
- 12—1½" squares

From black-and-tan toile, cut:
- 2—6¼×36½" outer border strips
- 2—6¼×35" outer border strips
- 8—7" squares, cutting each diagonally twice in an X for 32 setting triangles total (you will use 30)
- 6—3¾" squares, cutting each in half diagonally for 12 corner triangles total

continued

Assemble Blocks

1. For one block, gather one 2½" square and four 1⅞" squares from one light print and one 3¼" square and four 1½" squares from one black print or black-and-gold stripe.

2. Use a pencil to mark a diagonal line on wrong side of each light print 1⅞" square.

3. Align marked light print squares with opposite corners of black print or black-and-gold stripe 3¼" square. Referring to **Diagram 1**, sew a scant ¼" from drawn lines on both sides of lines. Cut apart on drawn lines to make two triangle units **(Diagram 2)**; press seams toward small triangles.

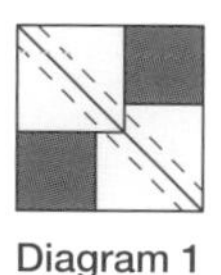

Diagram 1

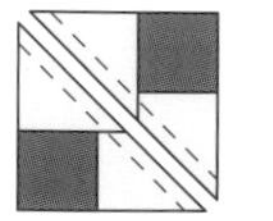
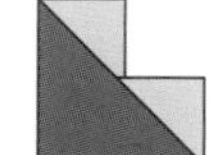

Diagram 2

4. Align a marked light print square with remaining corner of a triangle unit. Sew a scant ¼" from drawn line on both sides of line **(Diagram 3)**.

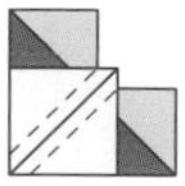

Diagram 3

5. Cut apart on drawn line **(Diagram 4)**; press seams toward small triangles to make two Flying Geese units. Each unit should be 2½×1½" including seam allowances.

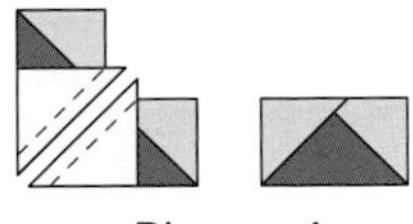
Diagram 4

6. Repeat steps 4 and 5 with remaining triangle unit to make four Flying Geese units total.

7. Sew together black print or black-and-gold stripe 1½" squares, Flying Geese units, and light print 2½" square in three rows **(Diagram 5).** Press seams toward squares in each row. Join rows to make an Evening Star block; press seams in one direction. The block should be 4½" square including seam allowances.

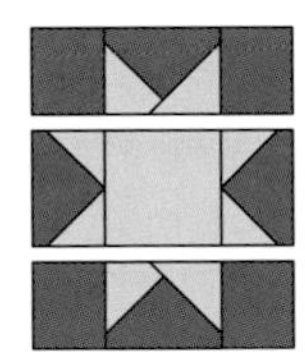
Diagram 5

8. To reduce bulk, clip through both layers of seam allowances up to seam lines ¼" on each side of seam intersections (clips will be ½" apart). Press center sections of seam allowances toward light print square and outside sections of seam allowances toward black squares. Press intersections open to create tiny Four-Patches **(Diagram 6).**

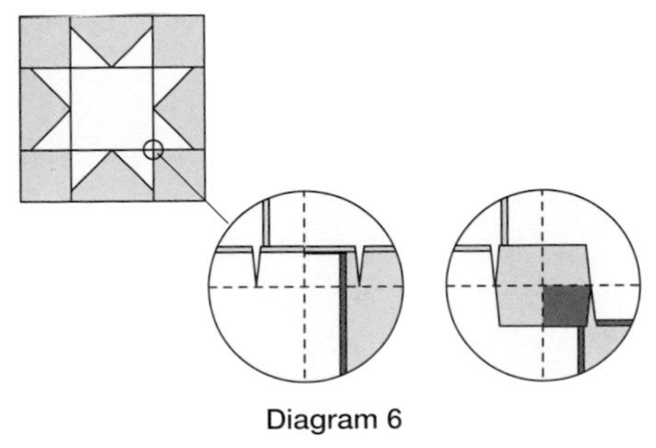
Diagram 6

9. Repeat steps 1–8 to make 18 Evening Star blocks total.

Assemble Block Rows

1. Referring to left-hand row in **Quilt Assembly Diagram**, lay out six Evening Star blocks, 10 black-and-tan toile setting triangles, and four black-and-tan toile corner triangles in diagonal rows.

continued

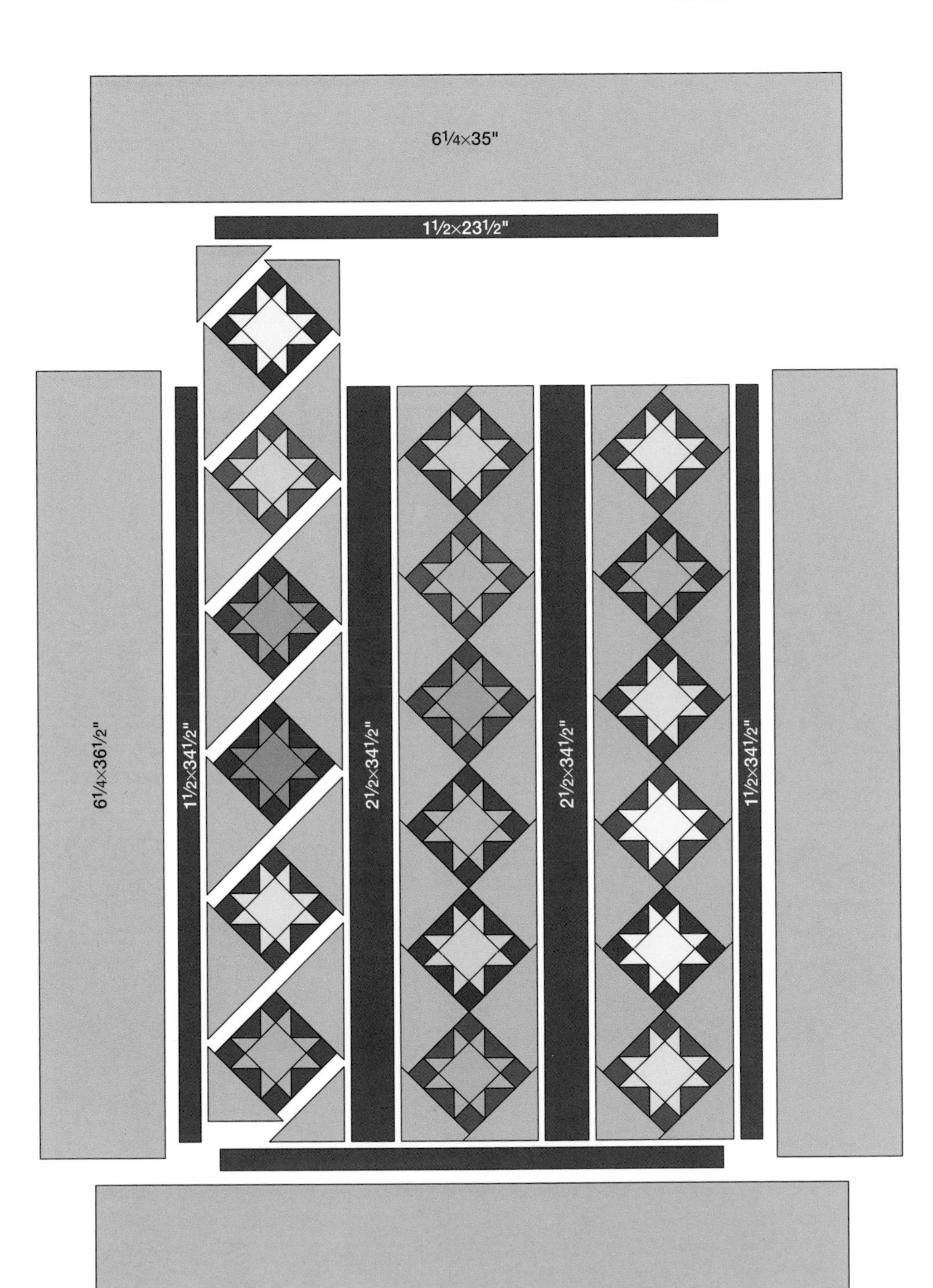

Quilt Assembly Diagram

2. Add setting triangles to opposite edges of block in each diagonal row (left row in **Quilt Assembly Diagram**). Triangle points will extend past adjacent edges of block. Press seams toward setting triangles.

3. Join diagonal rows. To reduce bulk, clip seam intersections as in Assemble Blocks, Step 8, *page 61,* and press seams toward setting triangles.

4. Add corner triangles, centering blocks on long edges of triangles, to make a block row. Press seams toward corner triangles.

5. Repeat steps 1–4 to make three block rows total.

Assemble Quilt Top

1. Referring to **Quilt Assembly Diagram**, join block rows and black-and-gold stripe sashing strips to make quilt center. Press seams toward sashing strips. The quilt center should be 21½×34½" including seam allowances.

2. Sew long black-and-gold stripe inner border strips to long edges of quilt center. Add short black-and-gold stripe inner border strips to remaining edges. Press all seams toward inner border.

3. Sew long black-and-tan toile outer border strips to long edges of quilt center. Add short black-and-tan toile outer border strips to remaining edges to complete quilt top. Press all seams toward outer border.

Finish Quilt

1. Layer quilt top, batting, and backing; baste. (For details, see Complete Quilt, *page 159.*)

2. Quilt as desired. Jo Richards stitched in the ditch around each block and sashing strip **(Quilting Diagram).** In the block centers, she stitched an orange peel design. She machine-quilted a feathered vine in the outer border, mimicking a portion of the design in each setting and corner triangle.

Quilting Diagram

3. Bind with black-and-gold stripe binding strips. For double-fold binding instructions, see Complete Quilt. For single-fold binding, attach binding strip to quilt in one layer, turning corners as in Complete Quilt. Turn binding to wrong side, fold raw edge of strip under ¼", and hand-stitch to backing.

optional colors

Touch of Royalty

This rich, dark table runner makes a great housewarming gift that comes together quickly. Quilt tester Laura Boehnke selected navy and burgundy fabrics to use in her small version of *Midnight Garden.*

"I made five Evening Star blocks, setting off the star in each with a neutral print," Laura says. To complete the table runner, she added 1"- and 4¼"-wide borders. The wide outer border utilizes the same bold floral as the setting triangles.

STRIPPY SOLIDS BED QUILT

A simplified design and an Amish-inspired color palette unite in a queen bed-size quilt.

Materials

- 2⅝ yards total assorted solids in purple, brown, blue, orange, black, pink, and green (block rows)
- 3 yards solid blue (setting and corner triangles)
- 2½ yards solid purple (sashing, inner border)
- 2⅝ yards solid green (outer border)
- ⅞ yard solid brown (binding)
- 8⅛ yards backing fabric
- 97×107" batting

Finished quilt: 88¾×99"

continued

Cut Fabrics

Cut pieces in the following order. Cut sashing, inner border, and outer border strips lengthwise (parallel to the selvages).

From assorted solids, cut:
- 150—4½" squares

From solid blue, cut:
- 70—7" squares, cutting each diagonally twice in an X for 280 setting triangles total
- 20—3¾" squares, cutting each in half diagonally for 40 corner triangles total

From solid purple, cut:
- 9—2½×85½" sashing strips
- 2—1½×85½" inner border strips
- 2—1½×77¼" inner border strips

From solid green, cut:
- 2—6¼×88¾" outer border strips
- 2—6¼×87½" outer border strips

From solid brown, cut:
- 10—2½×42" binding strips

Assemble Block Rows

1. Referring to left row in **Quilt Assembly Diagram**, lay out 15 assorted solid 4½" squares, 28 solid blue setting triangles, and four solid blue corner triangles in diagonal rows.

2. Referring to Assemble Block Rows, steps 2–4, *page 62*, join pieces to make a block row.

3. Repeat steps 1 and 2 to make 10 block rows total.

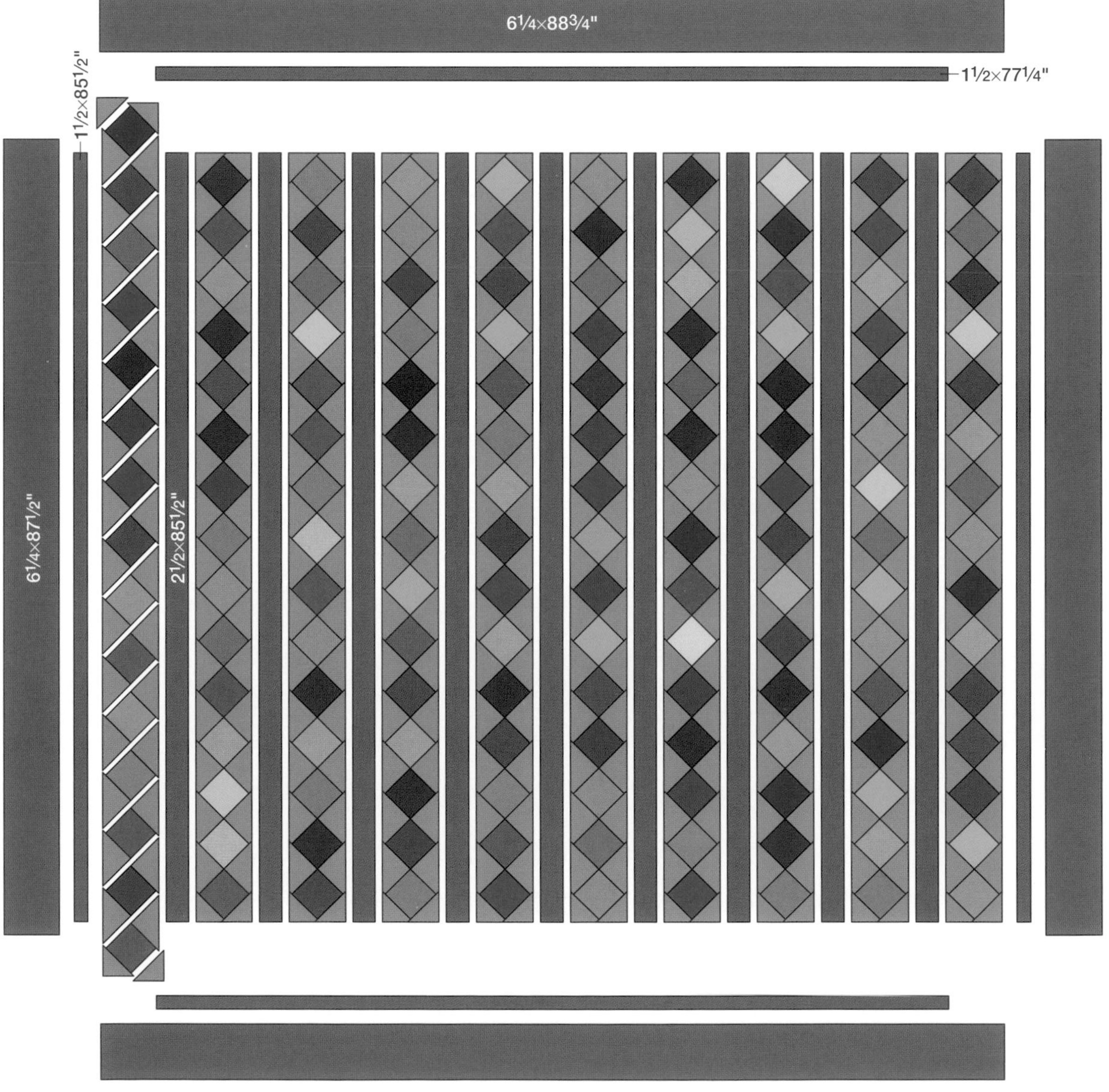

Quilt Assembly Diagram

Assemble Quilt Top

1. Referring to **Quilt Assembly Diagram**, *opposite,* join block rows and solid purple sashing strips to make quilt center. Press seams toward sashing strips. The quilt center should be 75¼×85½" including seam allowances.

2. Sew solid purple 1½×85½" inner border strips to side edges of quilt center. Add solid purple 1½×77¼" inner border strips to remaining edges. Press all seams toward inner border.

3. Sew solid green 6¼×87½" outer border strips to long edges of quilt center. Add solid green 6¼×88¾" outer border strips to remaining edges to complete quilt top. Press all seams toward outer border.

Finish Quilt

1. Layer quilt top, batting, and backing; baste. (For details, see Complete Quilt, *page 159.*)

2. Quilt as desired. The featured quilt is machine-quilted with a variety of feathered vine motifs.

3. Bind with solid brown binding strips. (For details, see Complete Quilt.)

ALL-STAR MINI QUILT

Set star blocks side by side to make a small quilt.

Materials

1/3 yard blue print (binding)

1/2 yard total assorted blue shirtings (blocks)

3/8 yard total assorted light shirtings (blocks)

3/8 yard total assorted red shirtings (blocks)

7/8 yard backing fabric

29" square batting

Finished quilt: 20½" square

Cut Fabrics

Cut pieces in the order that follows in each section.

From blue print, cut:

- 3—2½×42" binding strips

Cut and Assemble A Blocks

The following instructions result in one A block. Repeat cutting and assembly steps to make 13 A blocks total.

From one blue shirting, cut:

- 1—2½" square
- 4—1⅞" squares

From one light shirting, cut:

- 1—3¼" square
- 4—1½" squares

1. Use a pencil to mark a diagonal line on wrong side of each blue shirting 1⅞" square.

2. Referring to Assemble Blocks, steps 3–8, *pages 60* and *61,* use blue and light shirting squares to make an A block **(Diagram 7).**

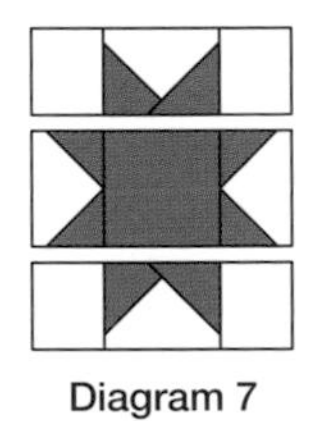

Diagram 7
Block A

Cut and Assemble B Blocks

The following instructions result in one B block. Repeat cutting and assembly steps to make 12 B blocks total.

From one light shirting, cut:

- 1—2½" square
- 4—1⅞" squares

From one red shirting, cut:

- 1—3¼" square
- 4—1½" squares

1. Use a pencil to mark a diagonal line on wrong side of each light shirting 1⅞" square.

2. Referring to Assemble Blocks, steps 3–8, *pages 60* and *61,* use light and red shirting squares to make a B block **(Diagram 8).**

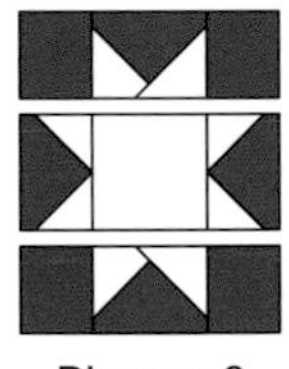

Diagram 8
Block B

Assemble Quilt Top

Referring to photo, *above,* sew together blocks in five horizontal rows, alternating A and B blocks in each row. Press seams toward B blocks. Join rows to complete quilt top. Press seams in one direction.

Finish Quilt

1. Layer quilt top, batting, and backing; baste. (For details, see Complete Quilt, *page 159.*)

2. Quilt as desired. The featured quilt is hand-quilted in red thread with an X through the center of each block.

3. Bind with blue print binding strips. (For details, see Complete Quilt.)

80
70
75
88

BOLD & BEAUTIFUL

Are you crazy about color? Do you delight in using bold prints? Combine an assortment of brightly hued fabrics and transform traditional shapes into stunning contemporary quilts. Experiment with color placement and discover new designs. The possibilities are endless!

RING OF *Fire*

Designer Barbara Brackman stitched fiery fabrics behind a dark grid to commemorate the day firefighters saved an Overland Park, Kansas, quilt shop from ruin.

Materials

16—18×22" pieces (fat quarters) assorted prints in red, pink, orange, yellow, and purple (blocks)

2¼ yards red-and-black print (blocks, sashing, outer border)

¼ yard blue print (blocks, sashing)

Scrap of solid blue

1 yard black print (inner border, binding)

4 yards backing fabric

70" square batting

Finished quilt: 61½" square
Finished block: 11" square

Quantities are for 44/45"-wide, 100% cotton fabrics. **Measurements** include ¼" seam allowances. Sew with right sides together unless otherwise stated.

SIZE OPTIONS: For a chart of optional sizes, turn to *Pattern Sheet 2*.

Designer Notes

Ring of Fire commemorates the day Harper's Fabric and Quilt Co. in Overland Park, Kansas, was almost destroyed. A fire devastated two businesses next door, but the quilt shop survived, and Harper's staff wished to acknowledge this near-tragedy with a special quilt. Historian and designer Barbara Brackman, a loyal customer, volunteered to come up with a design.

"I think it's always cathartic to commemorate and record important events with some kind of artwork," Barbara says. "I immediately thought of a circular design behind a grid, sort of like a fire in a grid of city streets. We talked about using all the very bright reds and oranges that are available, with a little blue to represent Harper's as the cool place in the middle of things."

Cut Fabrics

Cut pieces in the following order.

Patterns are on *Pattern Sheet 1*. To make templates of patterns, see Make and Use Templates, *page 157*. Mark or clip center of curved edge on each A and B piece. Be sure to transfer dots marked on patterns to templates, then to fabric pieces. These dots are matching points and are necessary when joining pieces.

From *each* fat quarter, cut:
- 4 *each* of patterns A and B

From red-and-black print, cut:
- 7—4½×42" strips for outer border
- 144—1½×5½" rectangles for blocks and sashing

From blue print, cut:
- 80—1½" squares for blocks and sashing

continued

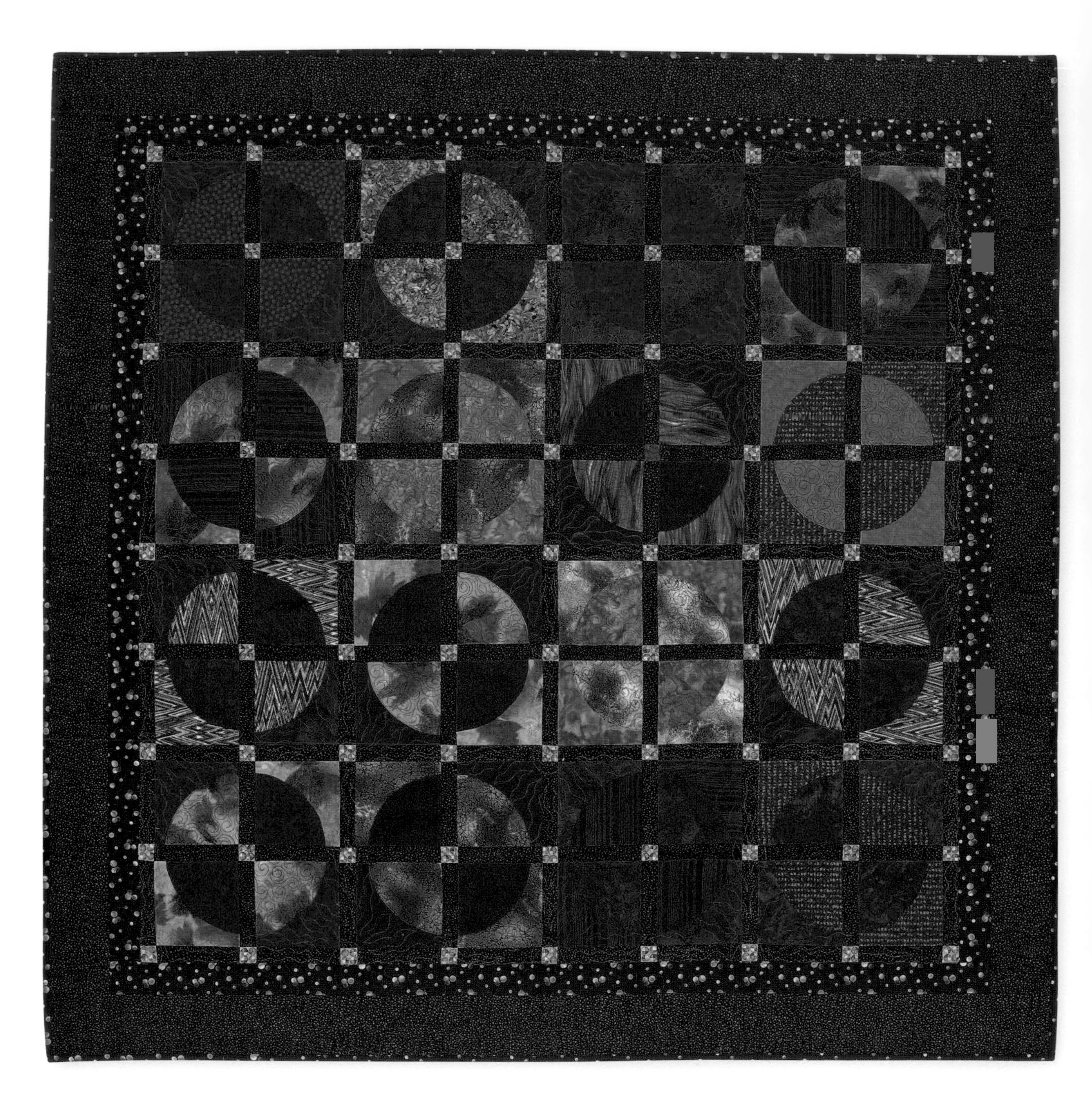

From solid blue, cut:

- 1—1½" square

From black print, cut:

- 12—2½×42" strips for inner border and binding

Assemble Blocks

1. For one block you'll need two A pieces and two B pieces from the same print, two A pieces and two B pieces from a second print, four red-and-black print 1½×5½" rectangles, and a blue print 1½" square.

2. Layer a B piece atop a nonmatching A piece; match center marks on curved edges **(Diagram 1)**.

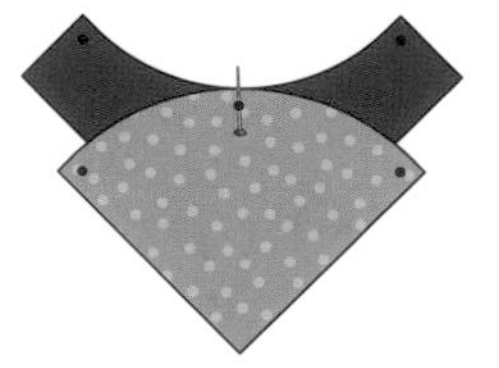

Diagram 1

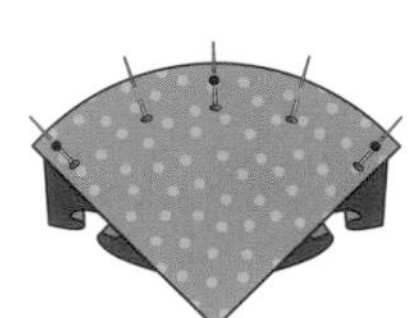

Diagram 2

3. Using slender pins and picking up only a few threads at a time, pin at center, then through matching points at each end; pin generously in between **(Diagram 2)**.

4. Sew together pieces, removing each pin just before your needle reaches it, to make a curve-pieced unit **(Diagram 3)**. Clip A piece's seam allowance as necessary (see Tip, *below*). Press seam toward A piece. The unit should be 5½" square including seam allowances.

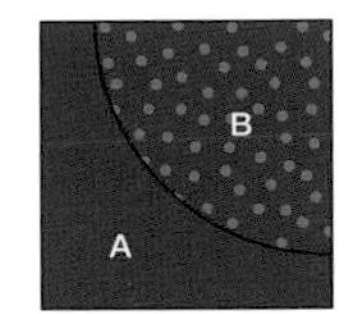

Diagram 3

5. Repeat steps 2–4 to make a matching curve-pieced unit.

6. Using remaining A and B pieces from Step 1, repeat steps 2–4 to make two reverse-color curve-pieced units.

7. Referring to **Diagram 4**, lay out curve-pieced units, red-and-black print 1½×5½" rectangles, and blue print 1½" square in three rows. Sew together pieces in each row. Press seams toward rectangles.

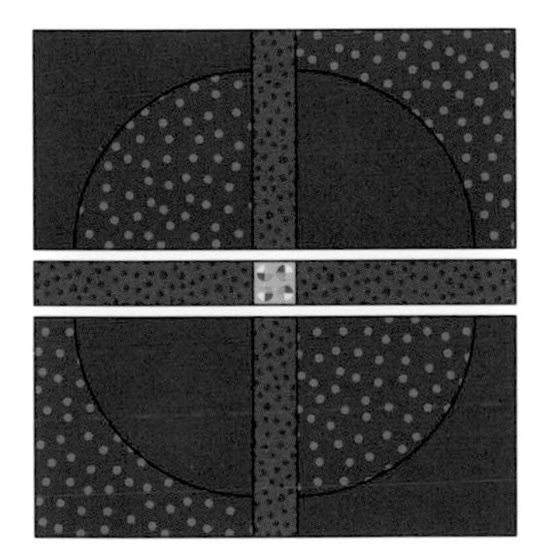

Diagram 4

8. Join rows to make a block. Press seams toward center row. The block should be 11½" square including seam allowances.

9. Repeat steps 1–8 to make 16 blocks total, using solid blue 1½" square in center of one block.

Assemble Quilt Center

1. Referring to **Quilt Assembly Diagram**, sew together two red-and-black print 1½×5½" sashing rectangles and a blue print 1½" sashing square to make a sashing unit. Press seams toward rectangles. The unit should be 1½×11½" including seam allowances. Repeat to make 20 sashing units total.

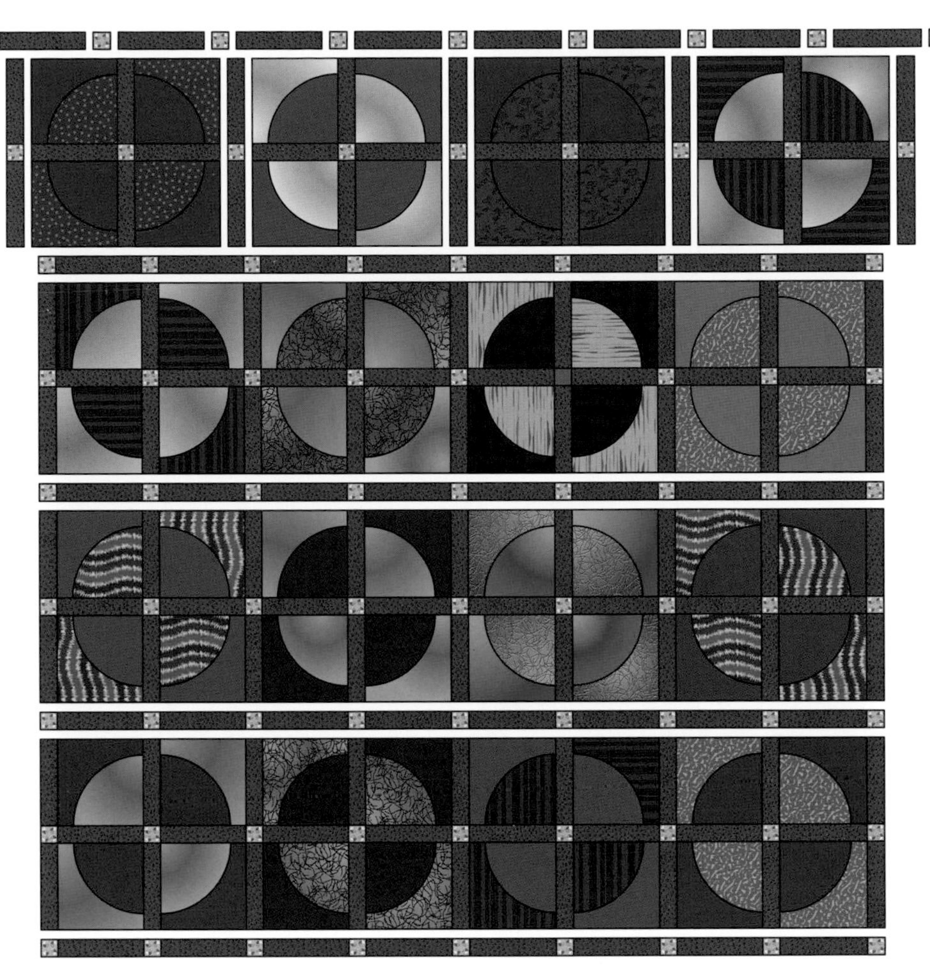

Quilt Assembly Diagram

2. Lay out blocks, sashing units, remaining red-and-black print 1½×5½" sashing rectangles, and remaining blue print 1½" sashing squares in nine rows **(Quilt Assembly Diagram)**.

3. Sew together pieces in each row. Press seams toward sashing units and rectangles.

4. Join rows to make quilt center. Press seams in one direction. The quilt center should be 49½" square including seam allowances.

continued

TIP: *Some quilters prefer not to clip curved seams. Instead they use a longer stitch length and sew slowly, which helps ease the fabric layers together.*

Quilting Diagram

Add Borders

1. Cut and piece black print 2½×42" strips to make:
- 2—2½×53½" inner border strips
- 2—2½×49½" inner border strips

2. Sew short inner border strips to opposite edges of quilt center. Add long inner border strips to remaining edges. Press all seams toward inner border.

3. Cut and piece red-and-black print 4½×42" strips to make:
- 2—4½×61½" outer border strips
- 2—4½×53½" outer border strips

4. Sew short outer border strips to opposite edges of quilt center. Add long outer border strips to remaining edges to complete quilt top. Press all seams toward outer border.

Finish Quilt

1. Layer quilt top, batting, and backing; baste. (For details, see Complete Quilt, *page 159*.)

2. Quilt as desired. Machine-quilter Karin O'Reilly stitched a swirling design in each circle and across the borders. She also quilted a free-motion flame motif radiating from every other sashing square **(Quilting Diagram).**

3. Bind with remaining black print 2½×42" strips. (For details, see Complete Quilt.)

optional colors

Safari Dance

Quilt tester Laura Boehnke used earth-tone batiks to create a piece that calls to mind the rhythmic tones of traditional African designs and prints. To unify her wall hanging, she used just two prints for the A pieces, alternating between cream and dark brown batiks.

"I like the way the border fabric echoes the curve-pieced units and contrasts with the straight lines of the grid and the crisp texture of the leaf prints," Laura says.

SEEING SPOTS THROW

Gentle curves make this an easy-to-sew quilt that comes together quickly.

Materials

13—18×22" pieces (fat quarters) assorted dark prints in blue, pink, yellow, aqua, purple, and green (blocks, binding)

13—18×22" pieces (fat quarters) assorted light prints in aqua, pink, green, purple, and yellow (blocks)

3⅓ yards backing fabric

59×79" batting

Finished quilt: 50½×70½" **Finished block:** 10" square

continued

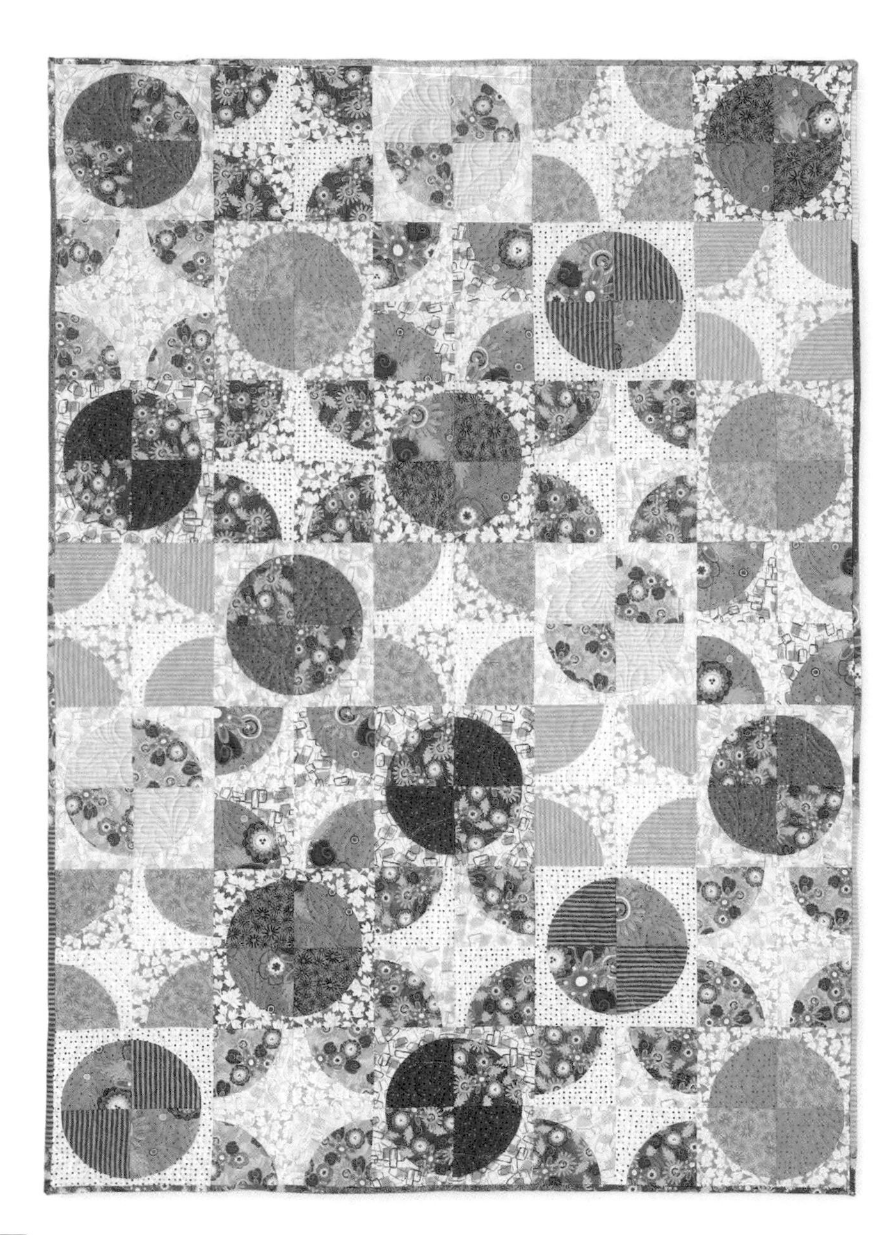

Cut Fabrics

Cut pieces in the order that follows in each section.

This project uses *Ring of Fire* patterns on *Pattern Sheet 1.*

From *each* assorted dark print, cut:

- 1—2½×22" binding strip

Cut and Assemble A Blocks

The following instructions result in one A block. Repeat cutting and assembly steps to make 18 A blocks total.

From one light print, cut:

- 4 of Pattern A

From *each* of two dark prints, cut:

- 2 of Pattern B

1. Referring to Assemble Blocks, steps 2–4, *pages 72* and *73,* use A and B pieces to make four curve-pieced units.

2. Referring to **Diagram 5**, sew together curve-pieced units in pairs. Press seams in opposite directions. Join pairs to make an A block; press seam in one direction. The block should be 10½" square including seam allowances.

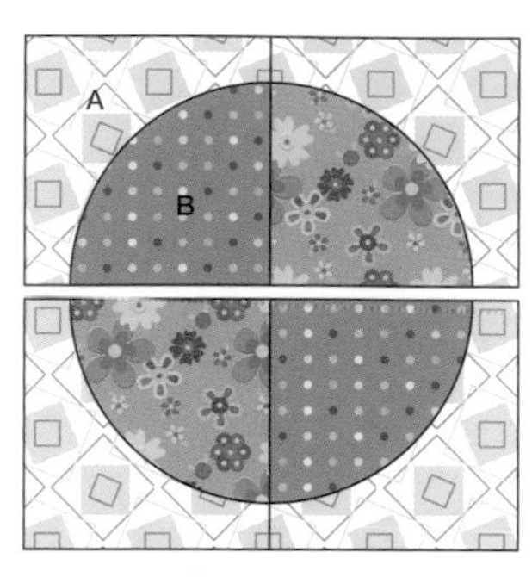

Diagram 5
Block A

Cut and Assemble B Blocks

The following instructions result in one B block. Repeat cutting and assembly steps to make 17 B blocks total.

From *each* of two light prints, cut:

- 2 of Pattern A

From one dark print, cut:

- 4 of Pattern B

1. Referring to Assemble Blocks, steps 2–4, *pages 72* and *73,* use A and B pieces to make four curve-pieced units.

2. Referring to **Diagram 6**, sew together curve-pieced units in pairs. Press seams in opposite directions. Join pairs to make a B block; press seam in one direction. The block should be 10½" square including seam allowances.

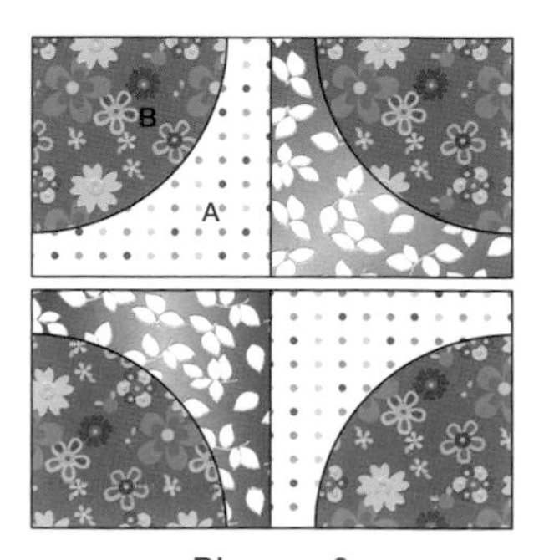

Diagram 6
Block B

Assemble Quilt Top

1. Referring to photo, *opposite*, lay out blocks in seven horizontal rows, alternating A and B blocks.

2. Sew together blocks in each row; press seams in one direction, alternating direction with each row. Join rows to complete quilt top. Press seams in one direction.

Finish Quilt

1. Layer quilt top, batting, and backing; baste. (For details, see Complete Quilt, *page 159.*)

2. Quilt as desired. The featured quilt was stitched with an allover feather design.

3. Using diagonal seams, sew together assorted dark print 2½×22" strips to make a pieced binding strip. Bind with pieced binding strip. (For details, see Complete Quilt.)

CHILD'S PLAY QUILT

Replace curve-pieced units from Ring of Fire *with novelty print squares.*

Materials

¼ yard *each* of yellow, teal, and red dots (sashing squares, binding)

¾ yard mottled dark blue (sashing rectangles)

42—5½" squares assorted novelty prints (blocks)

¾ yard mottled blue (border)

3 yards backing fabric

54×60" batting

Finished quilt: 45½×51½"

continued

Cut Fabrics

Cut pieces in the following order.

From *each* assorted dot, cut:
- 7—2½×10" binding strips

From *each* remaining yellow and teal dot, cut:
- 19—1½" sashing squares

From remaining red dot, cut:
- 18—1½" sashing squares

From mottled dark blue, cut:
- 97—1½×5½" sashing rectangles

From mottled blue, cut:
- 5—4½×42" strips for border

Assemble Quilt Center

1. Referring to **Quilt Assembly Diagram**, sew together seven yellow, teal, and red dot sashing squares and six mottled dark blue sashing rectangles to make a sashing row; press seams toward sashing rectangles. The sashing row should be 1½×37½" including seam allowances. Repeat to make eight sashing rows total.

2. Sew together seven mottled dark blue sashing rectangles and six assorted novelty print 5½" squares to make a pieced row **(Quilt Assembly Diagram).** Press seams toward sashing rectangles.

The pieced row should be 5½×37½" including seam allowances. Repeat to make seven pieced rows total.

3. Referring to **Quilt Assembly Diagram**, lay out sashing rows and pieced rows in 15 horizontal rows. Join rows to make quilt center; press seams in one direction. The quilt center should be 37½×43½" including seam allowances.

Add Border

1. Cut and piece mottled blue 4½×42" strips to make:

- 2—4½×51½" border strips
- 2—4½×37½" border strips

2. Sew short border strips to short edges of quilt center. Add long border strips to remaining edges to complete quilt top. Press all seams toward border.

Finish Quilt

1. Layer quilt top, batting, and backing; baste. (For details, see Complete Quilt, *page 159*.) Quilt as desired.

2. Using straight seams, sew together yellow, teal, and red dot 2½×10" strips to make a pieced binding strip. Bind with pieced binding strip. (For details, see Complete Quilt.)

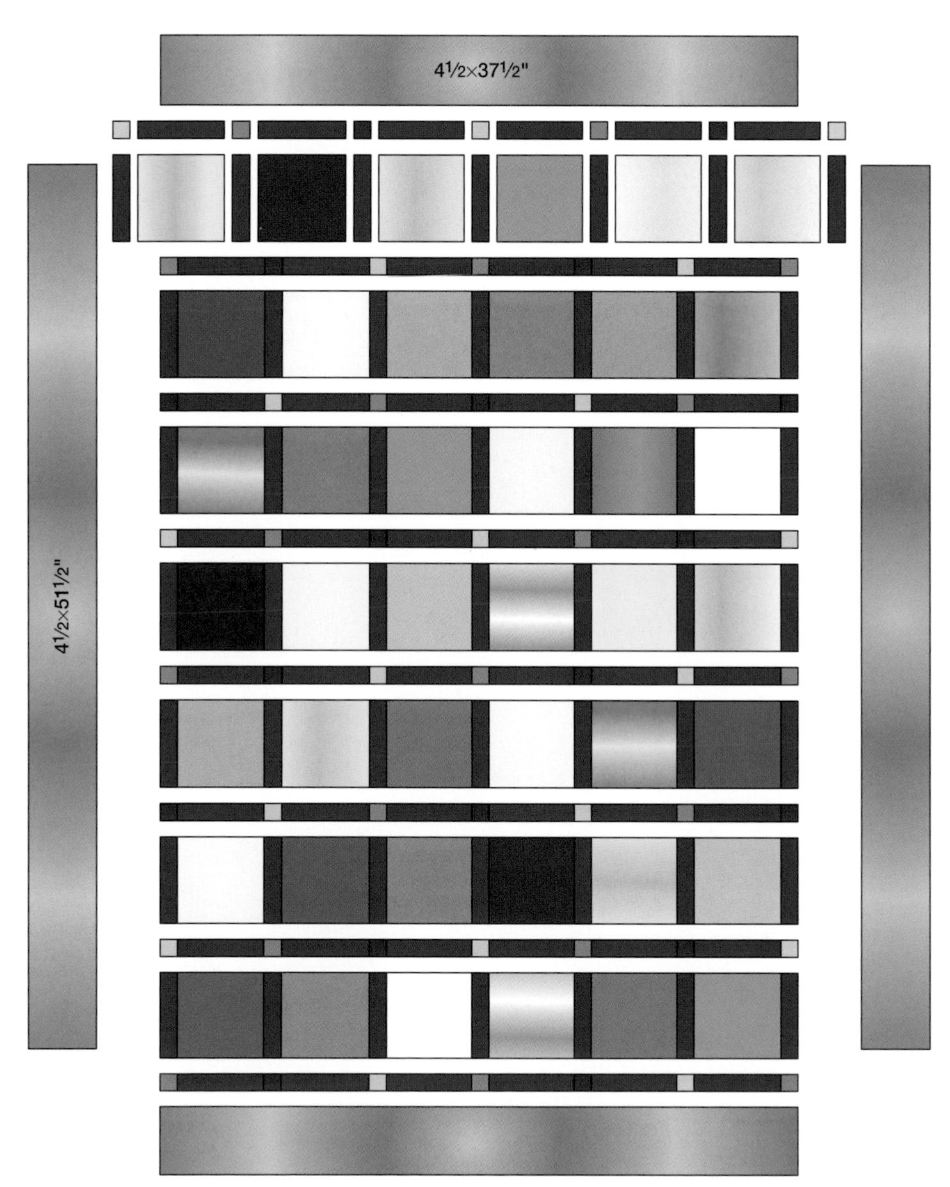

Quilt Assembly Diagram

COLOR *Cues*

Playing with color doesn't have to be a major production. Designer Amy Walsh auditioned an array of saturated solids to star in the framed rectangles of this easy-to-piece throw.

Materials

2⅓ yards total assorted bright solids (blocks)

2¼ yards solid white (blocks)

4 yards solid teal (sashing, border, binding)

7⅛ yards backing fabric

85×97" batting

Finished quilt: 76½×89"
Finished block: 6×8½"

Quantities are for 44/45"-wide, 100% cotton fabrics. **Measurements** include ¼" seam allowances. Sew with right sides together unless otherwise stated.

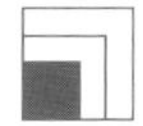

SIZE OPTIONS: For a chart of optional sizes, turn to *Pattern Sheet 2*.

Designer Notes

"This design and its colors are inspired by my husband, a Chicago stagehand," designer Amy Walsh says. "We frequently meet downtown by the stage doors. Each block in this quilt is one of those doors."

Amy, who enjoys working with solid fabrics, says she's quickly becoming a "solids addict." She recommends piecing a favorite pattern in solids. "You'll be amazed how it changes the look, plus there's no substitute when it comes to practicing your color expertise," she says.

Amy recommends washing all fabrics prior to sewing—especially if you are using solid white for the frame on each block. "I use ReTayne (a chemical fabric dye fixative) to wash solids before cutting and sewing," Amy says.

Cut Fabrics

Cut pieces in the following order.

From assorted bright solids, cut:
- 144—4×5" rectangles

From solid white, cut:
- 144—1¼×7½" rectangles
- 144—1¼×6½" rectangles

From solid teal, cut:
- 9—5½×42" strips for border
- 9—2½×42" binding strips
- 12—2×42" strips for sashing
- 64—2×9" sashing rectangles

Assemble Blocks

1. Aligning long edges, sew together two assorted bright solid 4×5" rectangles to make a block center **(Diagram 1)**. Press seam in one direction. The block center should be 5×7½" including seam allowances. Repeat to make 72 block centers total.

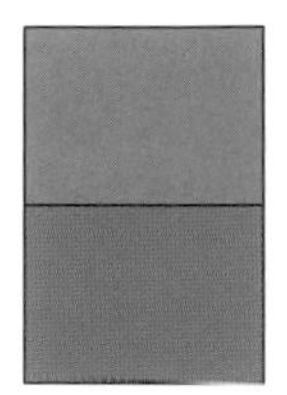

Diagram 1

continued

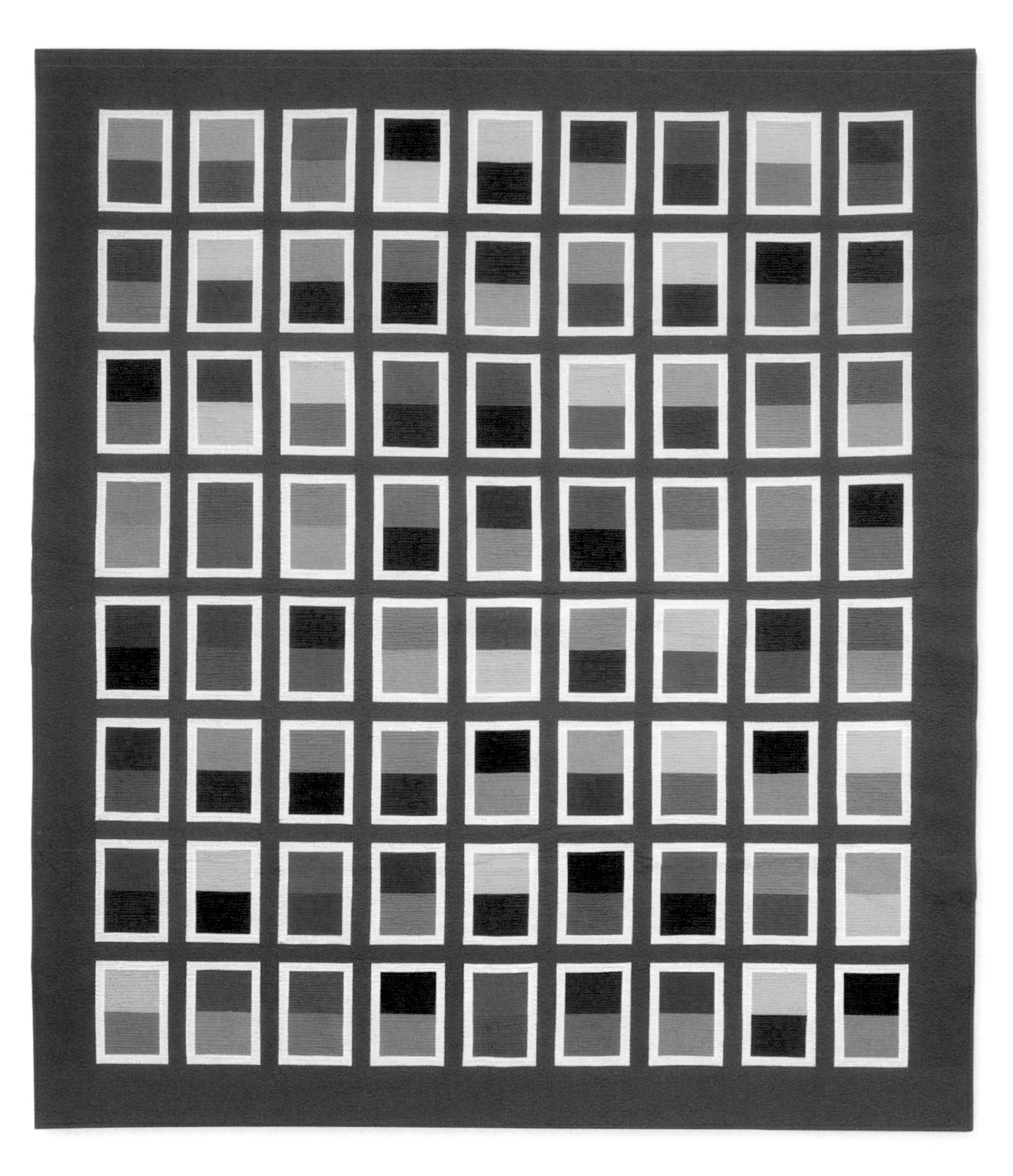

2. Sew solid white 1¼×7½" rectangles to long edges of a block center **(Diagram 2).** Add solid white 1¼×6½" rectangles to remaining edges to make a block. Press all seams toward block center. The block should be 6½×9" including seam allowances. Repeat to make 72 blocks total.

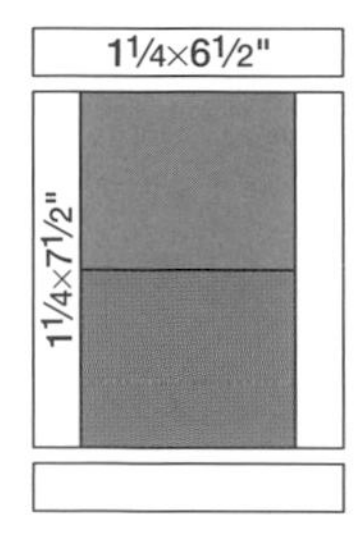

Diagram 2

Assemble Quilt Top

1. Cut and piece solid teal 2×42" strips to make:

- 7—2×66½" sashing strips

2. Referring to **Quilt Assembly Diagram**, lay out blocks, solid teal sashing rectangles, and sashing strips in 15 horizontal rows. Sew together pieces in each block row. Press seams toward sashing rectangles.

3. Join block rows and sashing strips to make quilt center. Press seams toward sashing strips. The quilt center should be 66½×79" including seam allowances.

4. Cut and piece solid teal 5½×42" strips to make:

- 2—5½×79" border strips
- 2—5½×76½" border strips

5. Sew long border strips to long edges of quilt center. Add short border strips to remaining edges to complete quilt top. Press all seams toward border.

Finish Quilt

1. Layer quilt top, batting, and backing; baste. (For details, see Complete Quilt, *page 159*.)

2. Quilt as desired. Amy machine-quilted an allover pattern resembling water ripples in the blocks and added stippling in the sashing and border **(Quilting Diagram).**

3. Bind with solid teal binding strips. (For details, see Complete Quilt.)

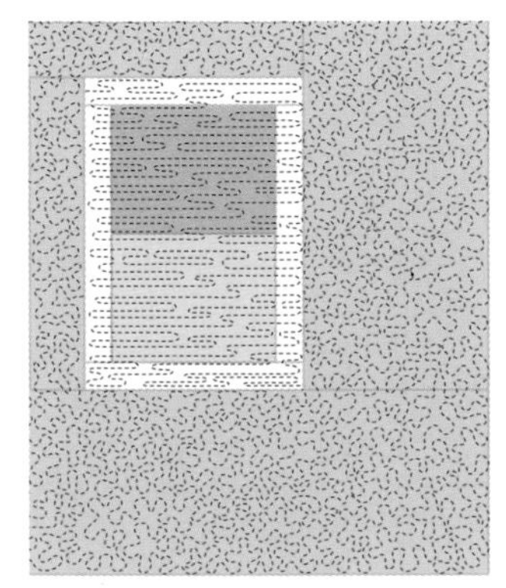

Quilting Diagram

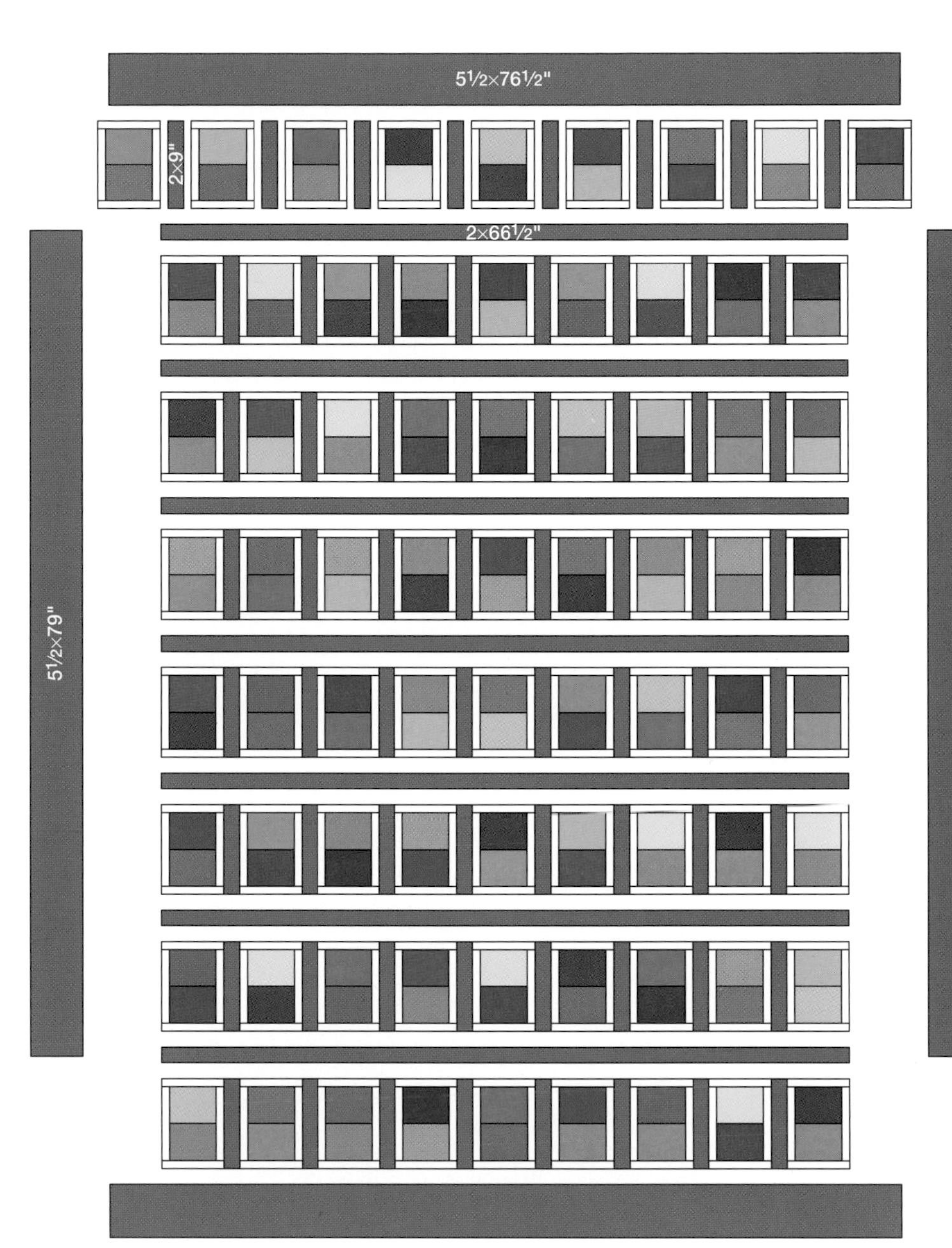

Quilt Assembly Diagram

optional colors

Role Swap

Reverse the position of light and dark found in *Color Cues* (try dark print rectangles around block centers with light-color sashing) to create another high-contrast quilt but with the opposite effect. If solids aren't your style, pair tone-on-tones with a bold floral to create block centers similar to those in quilt tester Laura Boehnke's wall hanging, *right*.

COURTYARD THROW

Showcase a large-scale print, medallion style, in the quilt center.

Materials

2⅓ yards total assorted prints in green, cream, brown, dark orange, gold, and red (blocks)

2⅓ yards dark green print (blocks)

⅝ yard gold paisley (center panel)

4 yards rust print (sashing, border, binding)

7⅛ yards backing fabric

85×107" batting

Finished quilt: 76½×99"

Cut Fabrics

Cut pieces in the following order.

From assorted prints, cut:
- 144—4×5" rectangles

From dark green print, cut:
- 2—1¼×27½" strips
- 2—1¼×21½" strips
- 144—1¼×7½" rectangles
- 144—1¼×6½" rectangles

From gold paisley, cut:
- 1—20×27½" rectangle

From rust print, cut:
- 9—5½×42" strips for border
- 9—2½×42" binding strips
- 14—2×42" strips for sashing
- 60—2×9" sashing rectangles

Assemble Blocks

1. Referring to Assemble Blocks, Step 1, *page 80*, use assorted print 4×5" rectangles to make 72 block centers total.

2. Referring to Assemble Blocks, Step 2, *page 82*, use dark green print 1¼×7½" and 1¼×6½" rectangles to make 72 blocks total.

Assemble Quilt Top

1. Sew dark green print 1¼×27½" strips to long edges of gold paisley 20×27½" rectangle. Add dark green print 1¼×21½" strips to remaining edges to make center block. Press all seams toward dark green print strips. The center block should be 21½×29" including seam allowances.

2. Cut and piece rust print 2×42" strips to make:

- 6—2×66½" sashing strips
- 2—2×29" sashing strips
- 4—2×21½" sashing strips

3. Referring to **Quilt Assembly Diagram**, lay out blocks, center block, rust print sashing rectangles, and sashing strips in 17 horizontal rows. Sew together pieces in each block row. Press seams toward sashing rectangles.

4. Join short block rows and 2×21½" sashing strips to make two block units. Press seams toward sashing strips. Sew together block units, 2×29" sashing strips, and center block to make center row. Press seams toward sashing strips.

5. Join long block rows, center row, and 2×66½" sashing strips to make quilt center. Press seams toward sashing strips. The quilt center should be 66½×89" including seam allowances.

6. Cut and piece rust print 5½×42" strips to make:

- 2—5½×89" border strips
- 2—5½×76½" border strips

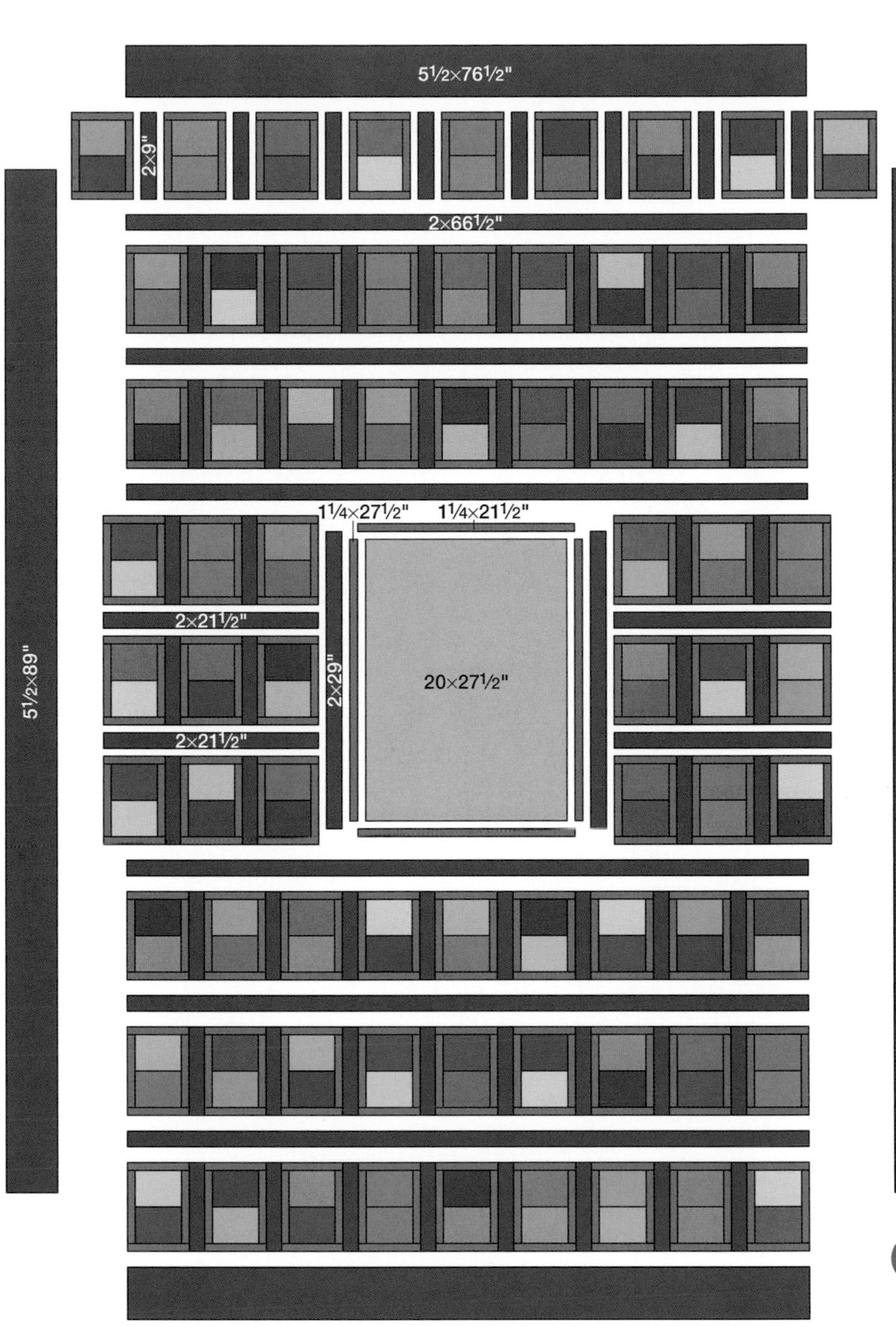

Quilt Assembly Diagram

7. Sew long border strips to long edges of quilt center. Add short border strips to remaining edges to complete quilt top. Press all seams toward border.

Finish Quilt

1. Layer quilt top, batting, and backing; baste. (For details, see Complete Quilt, *page 159*.)

2. Quilt as desired. Vertical lines are machine-quilted about ¼" apart in each block.

3. Bind with rust print binding strips. (For details, see Complete Quilt.)

PHOTO WALL QUILT

Preserve special memories on fabric.

Materials

11–8×11½" sheets of printer fabric (blocks)

7—9×22" pieces (fat eighths) assorted hand-dyed fabrics in dark brown, brown, light brown, light green, green, teal, and blue (blocks)

1⅛ yards solid black (sashing, border, binding)

1¾ yards backing fabric

63×40" batting

Finished quilt: 54½×32"

Plan Quilt

Following manufacturer's instructions, print desired photos onto printer fabric. The featured quilt includes 11 blocks with photos sized to fit 5×7½" rectangles, and 10 blocks with photos sized to fit 5×4" rectangles (two photos for each block). Rotate photos so you can print two 5×7½" photos or four 5×4" photos per sheet of printer fabric.

Cut Fabrics

Cut pieces in the following order.

From photos printed on printer fabric, cut:
- 11—5×7½" rectangles
- 20—5×4" rectangles

From *each* assorted hand-dyed fabric, cut:
- 6—1¼×7½" rectangles
- 6—1¼×6½" rectangles

From solid black, cut:
- 5—2½×42" binding strips
- 7—2×42" strips for sashing and border
- 18—2×9" sashing rectangles

Assemble Blocks

1. Referring to Assemble Blocks, Step 1, *page 80*, use photo-printed 5×4" rectangles to make 10 block centers.

2. Referring to Assemble Blocks, Step 2, *page 82*, use block centers and matching sets of hand-dyed 1¼×7½" and 1¼×6½" rectangles to make 10 two-photo blocks.

3. Repeat Step 2 using photo-printed 5×7½" rectangles and remaining matching sets of hand-dyed 1¼×7½" and 1¼×6½" rectangles to make 11 one-photo blocks.

Assemble Quilt Top

1. Cut and piece solid black 2×42" strips to make:
- 4—2×51½" sashing strips
- 2—2×32" border strips

2 Referring to **Quilt Assembly Diagram**, lay out blocks, solid black sashing rectangles, and sashing strips in seven horizontal rows. Sew together pieces in each block row. Press seams toward sashing rectangles.

3. Join block rows and sashing strips to make quilt center. Press seams toward sashing strips. The quilt center should be 51½×32" including seam allowances.

4. Sew solid black border strips to short edges of quilt center to complete quilt top. Press seams toward border.

Finish Quilt

1. Layer quilt top, batting, and backing; baste. (For details, see Complete Quilt, *page 159*.)

2. Quilt as desired. Parallel lines are machine-quilted about ½" apart in the solid black sashing pieces and border.

3. Bind with solid black binding strips. (For details, see Complete Quilt.)

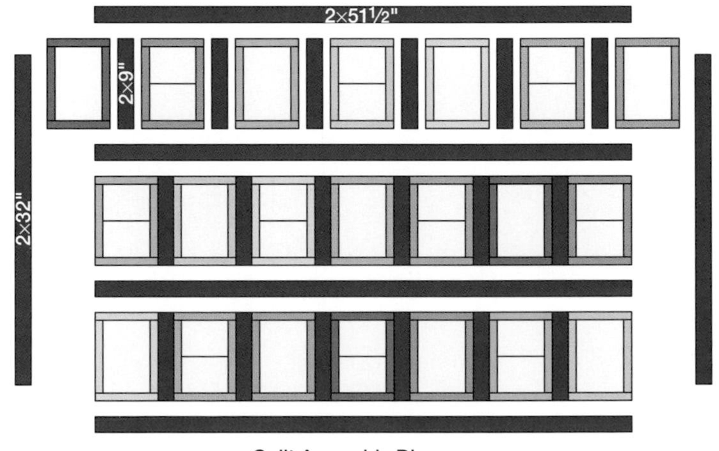

Quilt Assembly Diagram

COLOR *Burst*

Designers Angela Blair and Amy Fuehrer combined abundant florals and bold colors on this bed quilt, reminiscent of a lush, late-summer flower garden.

Materials

2⅛ yards black print (sashing, border Nos. 1 and 4)

⅔ yard solid teal (sashing squares, piping)

1¼ yards solid black (border No. 2, binding)

¾ yard *each* of solid burgundy, plum, rust, violet, red, and light orange (blocks, border No. 3)

½ yard *each* of solid olive, orange, gold, and lavender (blocks)

4 yards total assorted prints in red, green, blue, pink, lime, teal, and purple (blocks)

7⅝ yards backing fabric

91×103" batting

10 yards ⅛"-diameter cording

Finished quilt: 82½×94½"
Finished block: 12" square

Quantities are for 44/45"-wide, 100% cotton fabrics. **Measurements** include ¼" seam allowances. Sew with right sides together unless otherwise stated.

Cut Fabrics

Cut pieces in the order that follows in each section.

From black print, cut:
- 13—2½×42" strips for border Nos. 1 and 4
- 4—2×42" strips for border No. 1
- 49—1½×12½" sashing strips

From solid teal, cut:
- 1—22" square, cutting it into enough 1"-wide bias strips to total 360" in length for piping
- 20—1½" sashing squares

From solid black, cut:
- 9—2½×42" binding strips
- 8—1½×42" strips for border No. 2

From solid burgundy, cut:
- 21—2½×4½" rectangles
- 58—2½" squares

From solid plum, cut:
- 29—2½×4½" rectangles
- 38—2½" squares

From solid rust, cut:
- 22—2½×4½" rectangles
- 66—2½" squares

From solid violet, cut:
- 28—2½×4½" rectangles
- 44—2½" squares

From solid red, cut:
- 23—2½×4½" rectangles
- 56—2½" squares

continued

From solid light orange, cut:
- 29—2½×4½" rectangles
- 42—2½" squares

From solid olive, cut:
- 4—4½" squares

Cut and Assemble Shoo-Fly Blocks

Organizing your fabrics first before cutting them will make it easier to re-create this project. Pair up two different prints and one solid for each Shoo-Fly block. All of the solid colors except solid teal and solid black are used in the Shoo-Fly blocks.

The following instructions result in one Shoo-Fly block. Repeat cutting and assembly steps to make 30 blocks total.

From one solid olive, orange, gold, lavender, burgundy, plum, rust, violet, red, or light orange, cut:
- 2—4⅞" squares

From one red, green, blue, pink, lime, teal, or purple print (Print A), cut:
- 2—4⅞" squares
- 1—4½" square

From a second red, green, blue, pink, lime, teal, or purple print (Print B), cut:
- 4—4½" squares

1. Use a pencil to mark a diagonal line on wrong side of each solid-color 4⅞" square.

2. Layer a marked solid-color square atop a Print A 4⅞" square. Sew pair together with two seams, stitching ¼" on each side of drawn line **(Diagram 1).** Cut pair apart on drawn line to make two triangle units. Press each triangle unit open, pressing seam toward Print A, to make two triangle-squares. Each triangle-square should be 4½" square including seam allowances. Repeat to make four triangle-squares total.

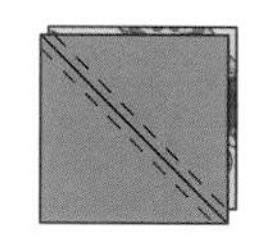

Diagram 1

3. Referring to **Diagram 2**, lay out triangle-squares, Print A 4½" square, and Print B 4½" squares in rows. Sew together pieces in each row. Press seams toward Print B squares.

Diagram 2

4. Join rows to make a Shoo-Fly block. Press seams in one direction. The block should be 12½" square including seam allowances.

Assemble Quilt Center

1. Referring to **Quilt Assembly Diagram**, lay out Shoo-Fly blocks, black print sashing strips, and solid teal sashing squares in 11 rows.

2. Sew together pieces in each row. Press seams toward sashing strips.

3. Join rows to make quilt center. Press seams toward sashing rows. The quilt center should be 64½×77½" including seam allowances.

Add Border Nos. 1 and 2

1. Cut and piece black print 2½×42" strips to make:
- 2—2½×80½" border No. 1 strips

2. Cut and piece black print 2×42" strips to make:
- 2—2×64½" border No. 1 strips

3. Sew short border No. 1 strips to short edges of quilt center. Add long border No. 1 strips to remaining edges. Press all seams toward border No. 1.

4. Cut and piece solid black 1½×42" strips to make:
- 2—1½×82½" border No. 2 strips
- 2—1½×68½" border No. 2 strips

5. Sew short border No. 2 strips to short edges of quilt center. Add long border No. 2 strips to remaining edges. Press all seams toward border No. 2.

Assemble and Add Border No. 3

1. Use a pencil to mark a diagonal line on wrong side of each solid burgundy, plum, rust, violet, red, and light orange 2½" square.

continued

Quilt Assembly Diagram

2. Align a marked solid 2½" square with one end of a solid burgundy, plum, rust, violet, red, or light orange 2½×4½" rectangle (**Diagram 3**; note direction of drawn line). Stitch on marked line and trim seam allowance to ¼". Press open attached triangle, pressing seam toward solid square.

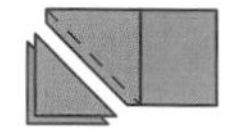 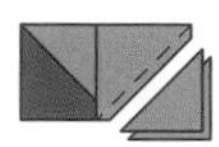 

Diagram 3

3. Align a second marked solid 2½" square with remaining end of Step 2 solid rectangle (**Diagram 3**; again note direction of drawn line). Stitch, trim, and press as before to make a Flying Geese unit. The unit should be 4½×2½" including seam allowances.

4. Repeat steps 2 and 3 to make 152 Flying Geese units total.

5. Referring to **Quilt Assembly Diagram**, *page 91,* join 35 Flying Geese units to make a short border No. 3 strip. Press seams in one direction. Repeat to make a second short border No. 3 strip.

6. Referring to **Quilt Assembly Diagram**, sew together 41 Flying Geese units in a row; press seams in one direction. Add a solid olive 4½" square to each end of row to make a long border No. 3 strip. Press seams toward solid olive squares. Repeat to make a second long border No. 3 strip.

7. Sew short border No. 3 strips to short edges of quilt center. Add long border No. 3 strips to remaining edges. Press all seams toward border No. 2. The quilt center now should be 78½×90½" including seam allowances.

Add Border No. 4

1. Cut and piece remaining black print 2½×42" strips to make:

- 2—2½×94½" border No. 4 strips
- 2—2½×78½" border No. 4 strips

2. Sew short border No. 4 strips to short edges of quilt center. Sew long border No. 4 strips to remaining edges to complete quilt top. Press all seams toward border No. 4.

Finish Quilt

1. Layer quilt top, batting, and backing; baste. (For details, see Complete Quilt, *page 159.*)

2. Quilt as desired. Machine-quilter Bobbi Gribble quilted parallel lines spaced ¼" apart across the prints of the Shoo-Fly blocks. She also stitched elongated loops in the solid-color triangles, creating a flower effect around the sashing squares. She quilted in the ditch in border No. 3 and accented the other borders with loops and waves.

optional colors

Bubble Gum Prize

Alluring shades of celery green, chocolate brown, and bubble gum pink evoke an air of sophistication in quilt tester Laura Boehnke's nine-block version of *Color Burst.*

"The brown-and-green botanical print made the sashing and border Nos. 1 and 4 a bit airy," Laura says. "To contrast with this, I chose a deep, dark burgundy for intensity in the sashing squares and border No. 2."

3. Cut and piece solid teal 1"-wide bias strips to make a 360"-long strip. Fold one strip end under 1½". With wrong side inside, fold strip in half lengthwise. Insert cording next to folded edge with a cording end 1" from strip's folded end. With a cording or zipper foot, baste through fabric layers right next to cording to make piping. Aligning raw edges, baste piping to quilt top, starting 1½" from piping folded end. As you stitch each corner, clip seam allowance to within a few threads of the stitching line; gently ease piping in place. After going around entire quilt top edge, cut cording end to fit snugly into folded opening; stitch to beginning point.

4. Bind with solid black binding strips. (For details, see Complete Quilt.) Be careful to keep cording out of the seam line when sewing binding on top of piping.

RED DELICIOUS

Mix together a variety of reds to make a scrappy two-color quilt.

Materials

4½ yards cream shirting (blocks, inner border)

1⅞ yards red floral (outer border, binding)

3⅞ yards total assorted red prints (blocks)

9 yards backing fabric

107" square batting

Finished quilt: 98½" square

Cut Fabrics

Cut pieces in the order that follows in each section. The featured quilt incorporates 49 assorted red prints—a different one for each block.

From cream shirting, cut:
- 9—1½×42" strips for inner border

From red floral, cut:
- 10—6½×42" strips for outer border
- 10—2½×42" binding strips

Cut and Assemble A Blocks

The following instructions result in one A block. Repeat cutting and assembly steps to make 25 A blocks total.

From cream shirting, cut:
- 2—4⅞" squares
- 4—4½" squares

From one red print, cut:
- 2—4⅞" squares
- 1—4½" square

1. Use a pencil to mark a diagonal line on wrong side of each cream shirting 4⅞" square.

2. Referring to Cut and Assemble Shoo-Fly blocks, Step 2, *page 90,* use marked cream shirting squares and red print 4⅞" squares to make four triangle-squares total.

continued

3. Referring to **Diagram 4**, lay out triangle-squares, red print 4½" square, and cream shirting 4½" squares in three rows. Sew together pieces in each row. Press seams away from cream shirting squares.

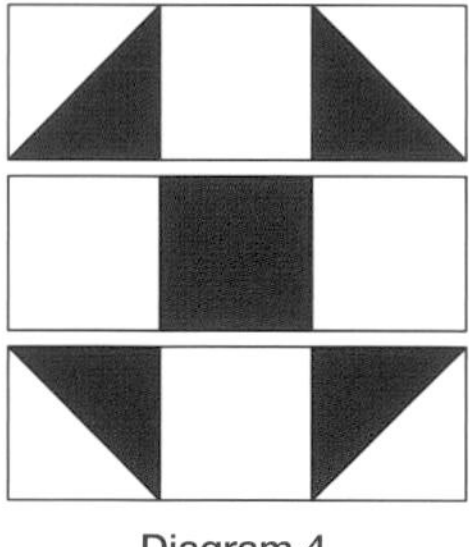

Diagram 4
Block A

4. Join rows to make an A block. Press seams away from middle row. The block should be 12½" square including seam allowances.

Cut and Assemble B Blocks

The following instructions result in one B block. Repeat cutting and assembly steps to make 24 B blocks total.

From cream shirting, cut:

- 2—4⅞" squares
- 1—4½" square

From one red print, cut:

- 2—4⅞" squares
- 4—4½" squares

1. Referring to Cut and Assemble A Blocks, steps 1 and 2, use cream shirting and red print squares to make four triangle-squares.

2. Referring to **Diagram 5**, lay out triangle-squares, cream shirting 4½" square, and red print 4½" squares in three rows. Sew together pieces in each row. Press seams toward red print squares.

3. Join rows to make a B block. Press seams toward middle row. The block should be 12½" square including seam allowances.

Quilt Assembly Diagram

Diagram 5
Block B

Assemble Quilt Center

1. Referring to **Quilt Assembly Diagram**, lay out blocks, alternating A and B blocks, in seven rows.

2. Sew together blocks in each row. Press seams toward B blocks.

3. Join rows to make quilt center. Press seams in one direction. The quilt center should be 84½" square including seam allowances.

continued

Add Borders

1. Cut and piece cream shirting 1½×42" strips to make:

- 2—1½×86½" inner border strips
- 2—1½×84½" inner border strips

2. Sew short inner border strips to opposite edges of quilt center. Add long inner border strips to remaining edges. Press all seams toward inner border.

3. Cut and piece red floral 6½×42" strips to make:

- 2—6½×98½" outer border strips
- 2—6½×86½" outer border strips

4. Sew short outer border strips to opposite edges of quilt center. Add long outer border strips to remaining edges to complete quilt top. Press all seams toward outer border.

Finish Quilt

1. Layer quilt top, batting, and backing; baste. (For details, see Complete Quilt, *page 159*.)

2. Quilt as desired. The featured quilt is stitched with an allover swirl-and-loop design.

3. Bind with red floral binding strips. (For details, see Complete Quilt.)

FLYING GEESE POT HOLDER

Piece Flying Geese units together for a quick-to-sew housewarming gift.

Materials for Gold Pot Holder

9×22" piece (fat eighth) gold print (Flying Geese units)

5" square red tone-on-tone (Flying Geese units)

9×22" piece (fat eighth) white print (Flying Geese units)

18×22" piece (fat quarter) multicolor stripe (binding)

11" square backing fabric

2—11" squares of batting

Finished pot holder: 8½" square

Cut Fabrics

Cut pieces in the following order.

From gold print, cut:
- 12—2½" squares

From red tone-on-tone, cut:
- 4—2½" squares

From white print, cut:
- 8—2½×4½" rectangles

From multicolor stripe, cut:
- Enough 2½"-wide bias strips to total 39" for binding (For details, see Cut Bias Strips, *page 157*.)

Assemble Flying Geese Units

1. Use a pencil to mark a diagonal line on wrong side of each gold print 2½" square and red tone-on-tone 2½" square.

2. Align a marked gold print 2½" square with one end of a white print 2½×4½" rectangle (**Diagram 6;** note direction of drawn line). Stitch on marked line and trim seam allowance to ¼". Press open attached triangle, pressing seam toward gold print.

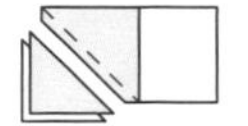
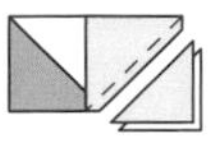
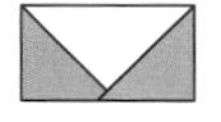

Diagram 6

3. Align a second marked gold print 2½" square with remaining end of Step 2 rectangle (**Diagram 6;** again note direction of drawn line). Stitch, trim, and press as before to make a gold Flying Geese unit. The unit should be 4½×2½" including seam allowances. Repeat to make four gold Flying Geese units total.

4. Using marked red tone-on-tone 2½" squares and remaining marked gold print 2½" squares, repeat steps 2 and 3 to make four red-and-gold Flying Geese units total **(Diagram 7).**

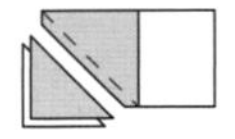
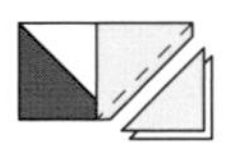
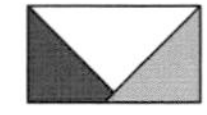

Diagram 7

Assemble Block

1. Referring to **Diagram 8**, sew together a gold Flying Geese unit and a red-and-gold Flying Geese unit to make a Flying Geese pair. Press seam toward red-and-gold Flying Geese unit. The pair should be 4½" square including seam allowances. Repeat to make four Flying Geese pairs total.

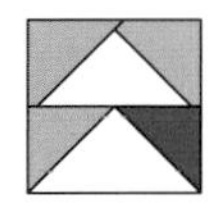

Diagram 8

2. Referring to **Diagram 9** for placement, lay out Flying Geese pairs in two rows. Sew together pieces in each row. Press seams in opposite directions. Join rows to make a block; press seam in one direction. The block should be 8½" square including seam allowances.

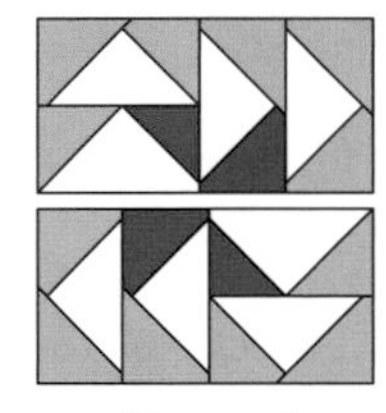

Diagram 9

Finish Pot Holder

1. Layer block, both squares of batting, and backing; baste. (For details, see Complete Quilt, *page 159*.)

2. Quilt as desired. The featured pot holder is stitched in the ditch of the white print triangles.

3. Bind with multicolor stripe bias binding strips. (For details, see Complete Quilt.)

Toss in a few different kitchen prints to make a complementary pot-holder gift set.

117
125
100
120

FUN WITH FAT QUARTERS

Whether purchased by the bundle or individually, fat quarters—18×22" pieces of fabric—are as necessary to a quilter's fabric collection as spices are to a cook's pantry. Form the right combination of "a little of this and some of that," by selecting fat quarters sorted by collection or color. Gather your stash of fat quarters and have fun planning the projects in this chapter.

PICK & *Choose*

Fabric bits and pieces are everywhere in this quilt, including the sashing, borders, and binding. Designer Carrie Nelson loved digging into her stash to come up with just the right mixture. The sashing may look complicated, but it's actually simple—just combine fabric strips, then trim to fit.

Materials

3⅔ yards total *or* 15—18×22" pieces (fat quarters) assorted light prints (blocks, border)

6¼ yards total *or* 30—18×22" pieces (fat quarters) assorted medium and dark prints (blocks, sashing, border, binding)

7½ yards backing fabric

87" square batting

Finished quilt: 78½" square
Finished block: 12" square

Quantities are for 44/45"-wide, 100% cotton fabrics. **Measurements** include ¼" seam allowances. Sew with right sides together unless otherwise stated.

Designer Notes

Particularly in scrappy quilts, designer Carrie Nelson prefers a pieced sashing and border to prevent any one fabric from dominating the overall design.

"If I had used a blue fabric for the sashing in *Pick & Choose*, it would appear to be a blue quilt even if there weren't any blue prints in the blocks," Carrie says. "And if I had cut sashing rectangles from the various fat quarters, some sashing strips would be more dominant because of a stronger color, print, or value." Keeping it all scrappy maintains a balanced look across the finished quilt top.

Cut Fabrics

Cut pieces in the following order.

From assorted light prints, cut:

- 100 sets of one 2×9" strip and one matching 3⅞" square
- 48—3⅞" squares (these are in addition to those just cut)
- 4—3½" squares

From assorted medium and dark prints, cut:

- 28—2½×14" binding strips
- 100—2×9" strips
- 286—1½×6½" rectangles
- 148—3⅞" squares

continued

Assemble Triangle-Squares

1. Use a pencil to mark a diagonal line on wrong side of each light print 3⅞" square.

2. Layer a marked light print square atop a medium or dark print 3⅞" square. Sew pair together with two seams, stitching ¼" on each side of drawn line **(Diagram 1)**.

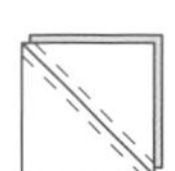
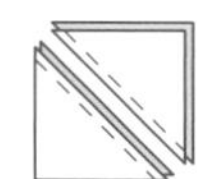
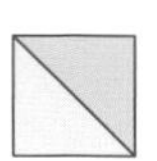

Diagram 1

3. Cut pair apart on drawn line to make two triangle units **(Diagram 1).** Open triangle units and press seams toward medium or dark print to make two matching triangle-squares. Each triangle-square should be 3½" square including seam allowances.

4. Repeat steps 2 and 3 to make 296 triangle-squares total (148 sets of two matching triangle-squares).

Assemble Four-Patch Units

1. Sew together a light print 2×9" strip and a medium or dark print 2×9" strip to make a strip set **(Diagram 2).** Press seam toward darker print. Cut strip set into four 2"-wide segments.

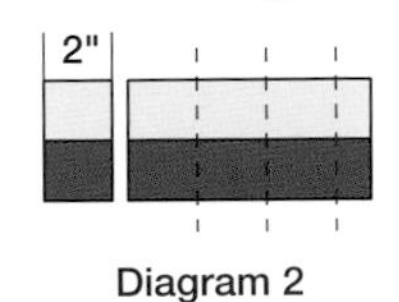

Diagram 2

2. Join two 2"-wide segments to make a Four-Patch unit **(Diagram 3).** To reduce bulk where multiple seams meet, Carrie suggests removing a few stitches at the seam intersection. Fan out seam allowances and press them flat, forming a tiny Four-Patch on the fabric wrong side **(Pressing Diagram).** Press seams in all units in same direction (clockwise in diagram shown) so seams will abut when units are joined together. The unit should be 3½" square including seam allowances. Repeat to make a matching Four-Patch unit.

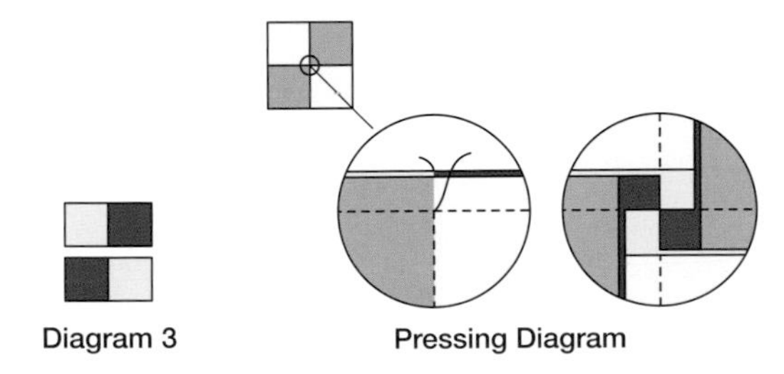

Diagram 3 Pressing Diagram

3. Repeat steps 1 and 2 to make 200 Four-Patch units total (100 sets of two matching units).

Assemble Blocks

1. For one Buckeye Beauty unit, gather two matching triangle-squares and two matching Four-Patch units, all with the same light print.

2. Referring to **Diagram 4**, lay out triangle-squares and Four-Patch units in pairs. Sew together pieces in each pair; press seams toward Four-Patch units. Join pairs to make a Buckeye Beauty unit; press seams clockwise as in Assemble Four-Patch Units, Step 2. The Buckeye Beauty unit should be 6½" square including seam allowances.

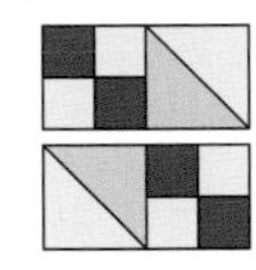

Diagram 4

3. Repeat steps 1 and 2 to make 100 Buckeye Beauty units total.

4. Referring to **Diagram 5**, lay out four Buckeye Beauty units in pairs, rotating units as shown. Join units in each pair. Press seams in opposite directions.

Diagram 5

5. Join pairs to make a block; press seams clockwise as in Assemble Four-Patch Units, Step 2. The block should be 12½" square including seam allowances.

6. Repeat steps 4 and 5 to make 25 blocks total.

continued

optional colors

Sunny Days

Quilt tester Laura Boehnke's light and bright version of *Pick & Choose* showcases playful prints in pastel shades.

"My personal fabric stash tends to be darker than this, so I don't always have the right fabric on hand if I want to make a light-color scrappy quilt," Laura says. If you have the same trouble, gather your friends for a fabric swap. By trading bits and pieces, you'll expand your stash without adding large pieces in colors you don't often use.

Assemble Sashing Strips and Rectangles

1. Sew together 13 assorted medium and dark print 1½×6½" rectangles along short edges to make a pieced strip **(Diagram 6).** Press seams in one direction. Repeat to make 22 pieced strips total.

2. Aligning long edges, lay out two pieced strips, offsetting them by about 3" **(Diagram 7).** Join pieced strips to make a pieced strip pair; press seam open. Repeat to make 11 pieced strip pairs total.

3. Trim ends of a pieced strip pair to make a 2½×72½" sashing strip **(Diagram 8).** Repeat to make six sashing strips total.

4. Cut each remaining pieced strip pair into six 2½×12½" segments **(Diagram 9)** to make 30 sashing rectangles total.

Assemble Quilt Center

1. Referring to **Quilt Assembly Diagram**, lay out blocks, sashing rectangles, and sashing strips in vertical rows. Sew together pieces in each block row. Press seams toward sashing rectangles.

2. Join block rows and sashing strips to make quilt center. Press seams toward sashing strips. The quilt center should be 72½" square including seam allowances.

Assemble and Add Border

1. Referring to **Quilt Assembly Diagram**, join 24 assorted triangle-squares to make a short border strip. Press seams in one direction. The strip should be 3½×72½" including seam allowances. Repeat to make four short border strips total.

2. Sew short border strips to opposite edges of quilt center. Press seams toward quilt center.

3. Sew assorted light print 3½" squares to each end of remaining short border strips to make two long border strips. Press seams toward light print squares. Add long border strips to remaining edges of quilt center to complete quilt top. Press seams toward quilt center. (To stabilize border for quilting, see Tip, *opposite*.)

Finish Quilt

1. Layer quilt top, batting, and backing; baste. (For details, see Complete Quilt, *page 159*.)

2. Quilt as desired. Diane Tricka machine-quilted the blocks with a swirl in each medium and dark print square, an X in each light print square, a feather motif in each medium and dark print triangle, and radiating lines across the light print triangles **(Quilting Diagram).** She also stitched in the ditch around the block units, sashing, and border, then added a continuous loop design in the sashing and a flame design in the medium and dark triangles of the border.

3. Using diagonal seams, join assorted medium and dark print 2½×14" strips to make a pieced binding strip. Bind quilt with pieced binding strip. (For details, see Complete Quilt.)

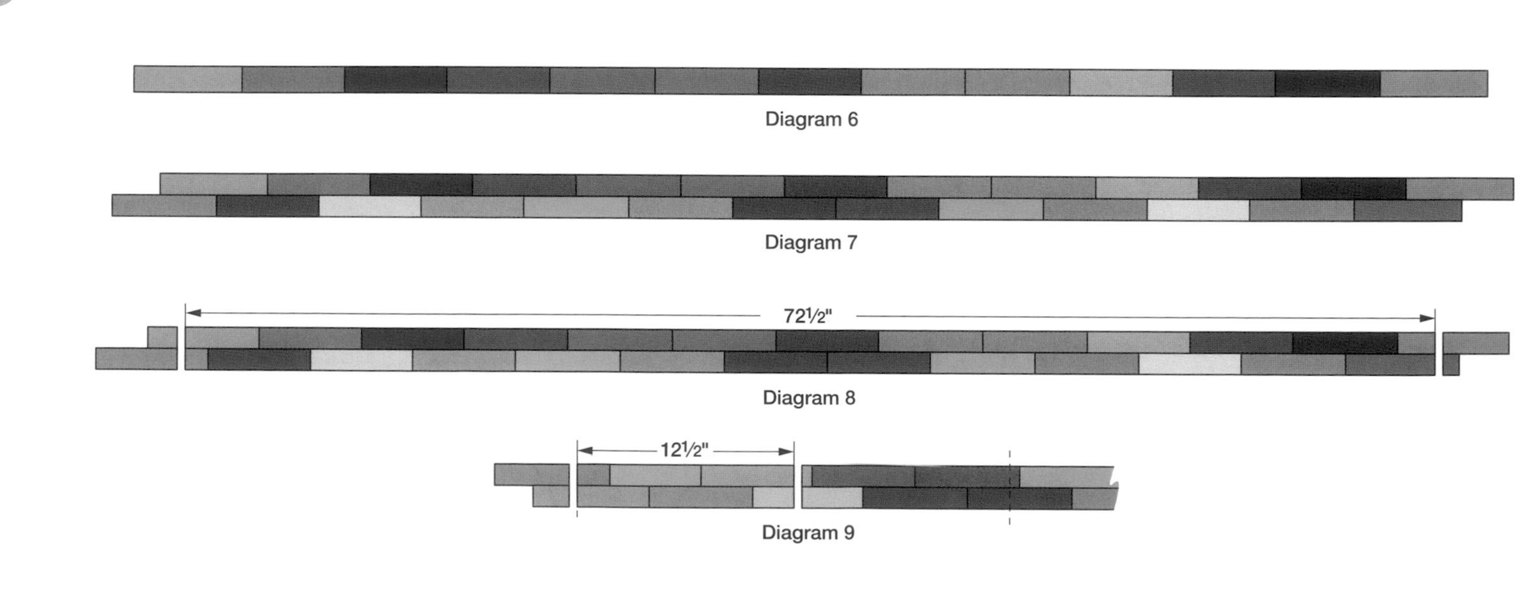

Diagram 6

Diagram 7

Diagram 8

Diagram 9

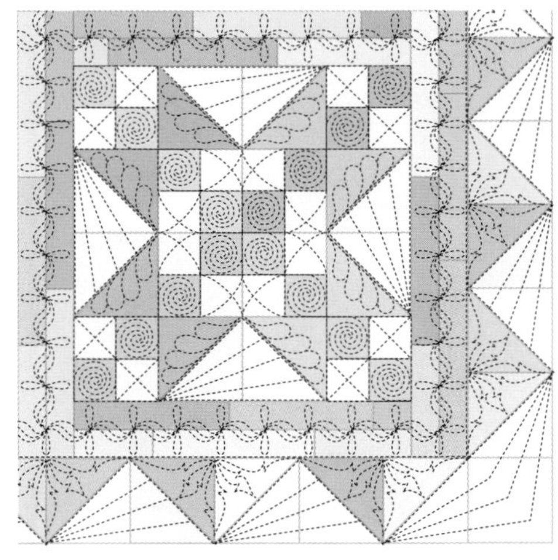
Quilting Diagram

TIP: *To prevent the pieced border seams from separating while you quilt and bind this project, machine-baste a scant ¼" from the outer edge around the entire quilt top. This will stabilize the border and keep your quilt in shape.*

Quilt Assembly Diagram

continued

POLKA-DOT APRON

Small scraps of dots are combined for a delightful apron that is sure to please the young and young-at-heart.

Materials

¼ yard total assorted dots (apron trim)

¾ yard cream dot (apron front, waistband)

⅝ yard muslin (apron lining)

Finished apron (length from waistband): 20½"

Cut Fabrics

Cut pieces in the following order.

From assorted dots, cut:
- 52—2" squares

From cream dot, cut:
- 2—4×40" strips
- 1—18×39½" rectangle

From muslin, cut:
- 1—21×39½" rectangle

Assemble Apron Trim

1. Sew together four assorted dot 2" squares in pairs. Press seams in opposite directions. Join pairs to make a Four-Patch unit; press seam in one direction. The Four-Patch unit should be 3½" square including seam allowances. Repeat to make 13 Four-Patch units total.

2. Referring to **Diagram 10**, lay out 13 Four-Patch units in a row. Sew together units to make apron trim; press seams in one direction. The apron trim should be 3½×39½" including seam allowances.

Diagram 10

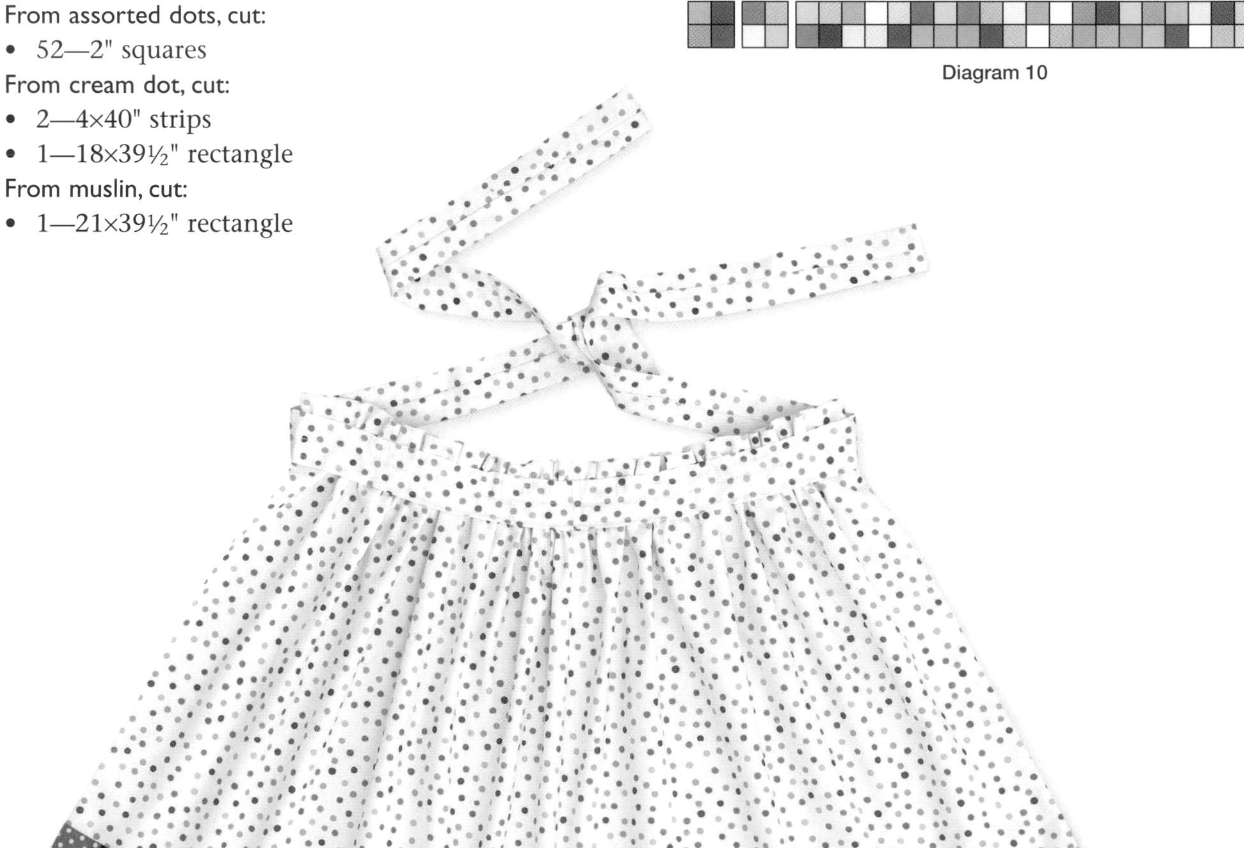

Assemble Apron Body

1. Sew together apron trim and cream dot 18×39½" rectangle to make apron front **(Diagram 11).** Press seam away from apron trim. The apron front should be 21×39½" including seam allowances.

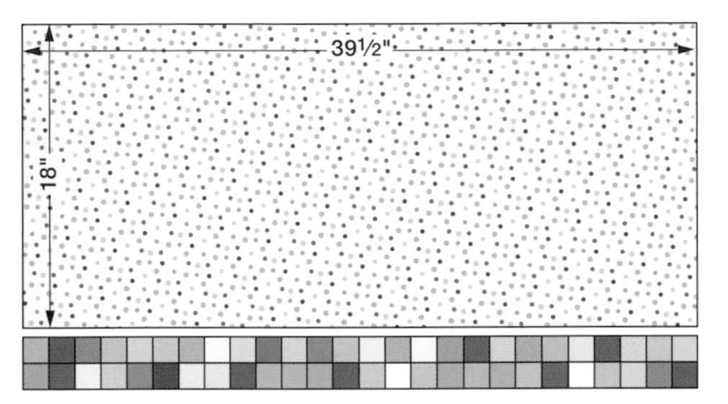

Diagram 11

2. With right sides together, join apron front and muslin 21×39½" rectangle, leaving a 3" opening for turning **(Diagram 12).** Trim corners.

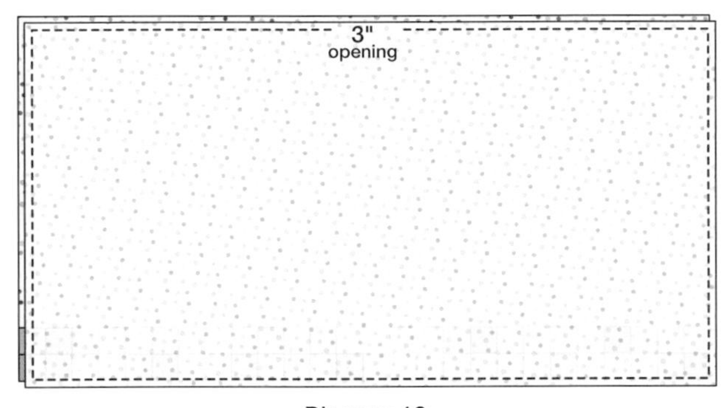

Diagram 12

3. Turn right side out. Whipstitch opening closed to make apron body. Press.

4. Machine-baste 1½" from top edge of apron body, stitching from one short edge to the other. Pull threads to gather top edge to desired width. Secure gathering threads (do not trim).

Finish Apron

1. Sew together two cream dot 4×40" strips along short edges to make a pieced strip. Press seam open.

2. With right side inside and aligning long edges, fold pieced strip in half. Lightly press; pin along long raw edges. Sew together long edges. Turn right side out. Refold strip, centering seam in back; press. Fold in raw edges ¼" at one short end and slip-stitch opening closed; press. Repeat with remaining short end to make waistband. The waistband should be 1¾×79".

3. Center and pin waistband to gathered edge of apron body, adjusting gathers evenly **(Diagram 13).** Topstitch waistband to apron body in three rows about ⅝" apart. Trim gathering threads to complete apron.

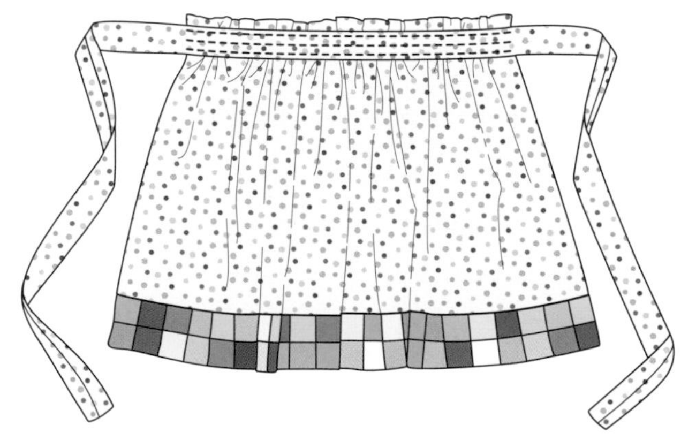
Diagram 13

SHADES OF THE SEA THROW

Myriad batiks in green, aqua, and blue surround a botanical print.

Materials

3 yards total assorted medium and dark batiks in aqua, green, and blue (sashing, border)

4¼ yards aqua floral (quilt center, binding)

1 yard total assorted light batiks in aqua, green, and blue (border)

7½ yards backing fabric

87" square batting

Finished quilt: 78½" square

Cut Fabrics

Cut pieces in the following order.

From assorted medium and dark batiks, cut:
- 286—1½×6½" rectangles
- 48—3⅞" squares

From aqua floral, cut:
- 8—2½×42" binding strips
- 25—12½" squares

From assorted light batiks, cut:
- 48—3⅞" squares
- 4—3½" squares

Assemble Sashing Strips and Rectangles

Referring to Assemble Sashing Strips and Rectangles, steps 1–4, *page 104,* use assorted medium and dark batik 1½×6½" rectangles to make six sashing strips and 30 sashing rectangles total.

Assemble Quilt Center

1. Referring to photo, *below,* lay out aqua floral 12½" squares, sashing rectangles, and sashing strips in vertical rows. Sew together pieces in each block row. Press seams toward sashing rectangles.

2. Join block rows and sashing strips to make quilt center. Press seams toward sashing strips. The quilt center should be 72½" square including seam allowances.

Assemble and Add Border

1. Referring to Assemble Triangle-Squares, steps 1–3, *page 102,* use assorted light batik 3⅞" squares and medium and dark batik 3⅞" squares to make 96 triangle-squares total.

2. Referring to Assemble and Add Border, steps 1–3, *page 104,* use triangle-squares and light batik 3½" squares to assemble and add border to quilt center.

Finish Quilt

1. Layer quilt top, batting, and backing; baste. (For details, see Complete Quilt, *page 159.*)

2. Quilt as desired. Swirl and wave designs are machine-quilted across the featured quilt top.

3. Bind with aqua floral binding strips. (For details, see Complete Quilt.)

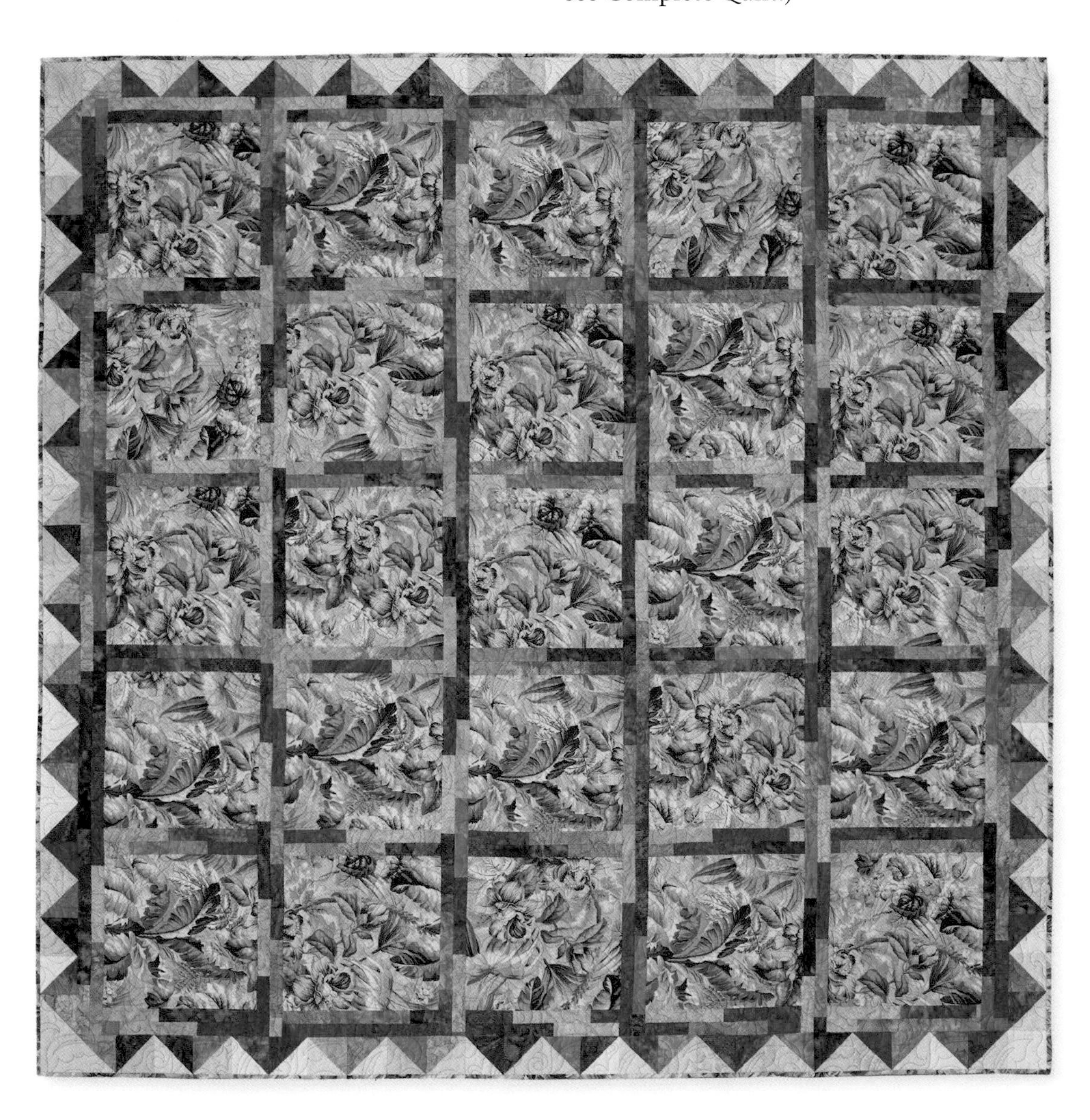

MODERN *Mix*

A traditional Hourglass or Four-X block is modernized with batiks and seemingly random strip sets. Look closely and you'll see there is indeed rhyme and reason behind the blocks in this energetic quilt from designer Mabeth Oxenreider.

Materials

32—18×22" pieces (fat quarters) assorted dark batiks (blocks)

32—18×22" pieces (fat quarters) light batiks in same colors as dark batiks (blocks)

7/8 yard violet-blue batik (binding)

7¾ yards backing fabric

93×105" batting

Finished quilt: 84½×96½"
Finished blocks: 6" square, 12" square

Quantities are for 44/45"-wide, 100% cotton fabrics. **Measurements** include ¼" seam allowances. Sew with right sides together unless otherwise stated.

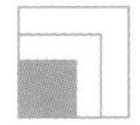

SIZE OPTIONS: For a chart of optional sizes, turn to *Pattern Sheet 2*.

Plan Block Colors

Designer Mabeth Oxenreider was careful to make each block with coordinating dark and light batiks. Instructions that follow are for the same effect.

Before cutting, pair up each dark and light batik. You'll work with four pairs of dark and light prints at a time to make a set of coordinating large and small blocks. Cut pairs of dark and light fat quarters at the same time; keep them stacked together so you don't forget which light goes with which dark.

Cut Fabrics

Cut pieces in the order that follows in each section. Patterns are on *Pattern Sheet 1*. To make templates of patterns, see Make and Use Templates, *page 157*.

Cut and Assemble A Blocks

Separate 20 dark batiks and 20 light batiks into five groups of four matching dark and light colors.

From *each* of one dark batik and its matching light batik, cut:
- 2—2⅝×22" strips
- 2—1¼×22" strips

From *each* of second dark batik and its matching light batik, cut:
- 2—2⅝×22" strips
- 2—1¾×22" strips

From *each* of third dark batik and its matching light batik, cut:
- 2—2½×22" strips
- 2—1¼×22" strips

From *each* of fourth dark batik and its matching light batik, cut:
- 2—2½×22" strips
- 2—1¾×22" strips

continued

1. Lay out a 2⅝×22" strip of dark batik No. 1, a 1¾×22" strip of dark batik No. 2, a 1¼×22" strip of dark batik No. 3, and a 2½×22" strip of dark batik No. 4. Sew together to make a dark strip set **(Diagram 1).** Press seams toward top strip. The strip set should be 6⅝" wide including seam allowances. Repeat to make a second, identical dark strip set.

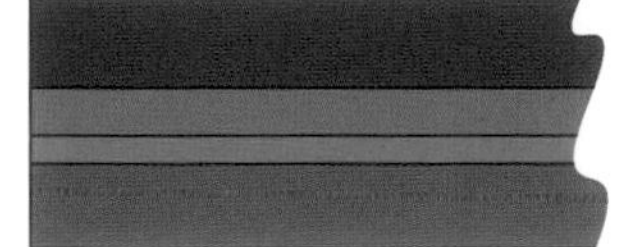

Diagram 1

2. Lay out four light batik strips the same colors and widths as those used in dark strip set. Join to make a light strip set **(Diagram 2)**. Press seams toward bottom strip. Repeat to make a second, identical light strip set.

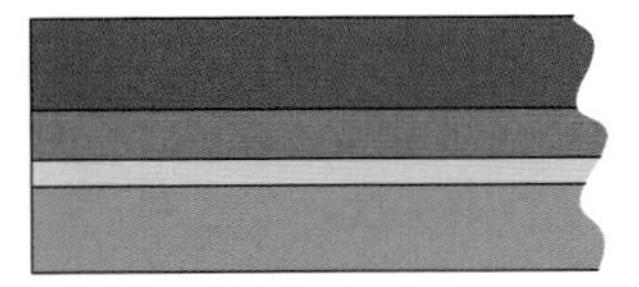
Diagram 2

3. Referring to **Diagram 3**, from *each* light and dark strip set, cut:

- 2 of Large Triangle Pattern
- 1 of Small Triangle Pattern

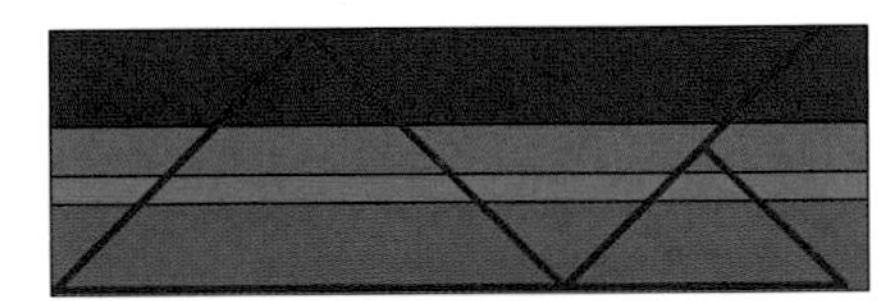
Diagram 3

4. Referring to **Diagram 4**, lay out two dark large triangles and two light large triangles that all have the same color at their base. Sew together large triangles in pairs; press seams toward dark triangles. Join pairs to make a large A block; press seam in one direction. The block should be 12½" square including seam allowances.

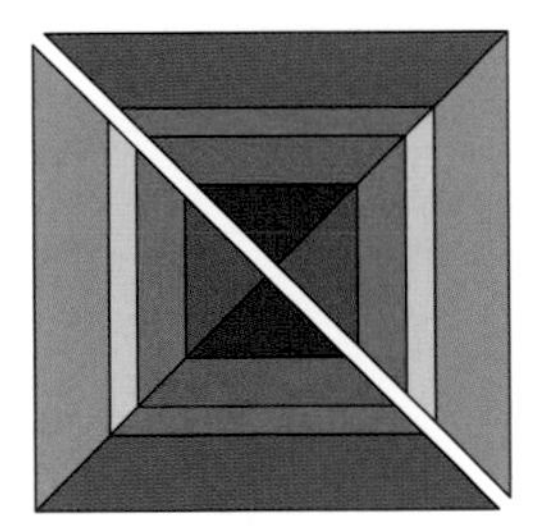
Diagram 4

5. Repeat Step 4 with remaining large triangles to make a second large A block; it will have the opposite color progression of the first block **(Diagram 5)**.

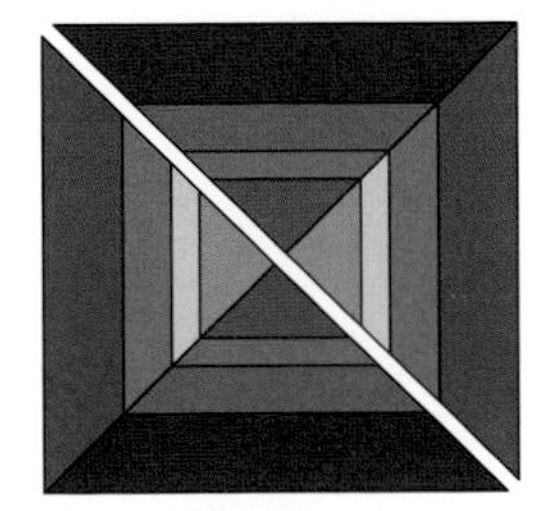
Diagram 5

6. Repeat Step 4 with small triangles to make a small A block **(Diagram 6)**. The block should be 6½" square including seam allowances.

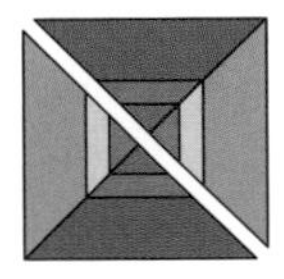
Diagram 6

7. Repeat steps 1–6 with remaining dark batik and light batik strips, mixing up the order of color and strip width as desired. You should now have four large A blocks and two small A blocks total.

8. Repeat cutting instructions and steps 1–7 with remaining dark and light batik groups to make 20 large A blocks and 10 small A blocks total.

Cut and Assemble B Blocks

Separate the 12 remaining dark batiks and 12 remaining light batiks into three groups of four matching dark and light colors.

From *each* of one dark batik and its matching light batik, cut:

- 2—3×22" strips
- 2—1⅝×22" strips

From *each* of second dark batik and its matching light batik, cut:

- 2—1⅝×22" strips
- 2—1½×22" strips

From *each* of third dark batik and its matching light batik, cut:

- 2—2×22" strips
- 2—1½×22" strips

From *each* of fourth dark batik and its matching light batik, cut:

- 2—3×22" strips
- 2—2×22" strips

1. Referring to Cut and Assemble A Blocks, Step 1, use 3×22" strips of dark batik No. 1, 1⅝×22" strips of dark batik No. 2, 1½×22" strips of dark batik No. 3, and 2×22" strips of dark batik No. 4 to make two identical dark strip sets. Press seams toward top strip in each set. Each strip set should be 6⅝" wide including seam allowances.

2. Referring to Cut and Assemble A Blocks, steps 2–7, make four large B blocks and two small B blocks.

3. Repeat cutting instructions and steps 1 and 2 with remaining dark and light batik groups to make 12 large B blocks and six small B blocks total.

continued

Cut and Assemble C Blocks

From *each* remaining dark batik scrap and its corresponding light batik scrap, cut:

- 22"-long strips in a variety of widths ranging from 1" to 2½"

1. Sew together enough dark batik strips to make a dark strip set at least 3⅝" wide. Press seams toward top strip. Repeat to make a coordinating light strip set with the same order of color and strip width. Press seams toward bottom strip.

2. Repeat Step 1 to make 40 pairs of light and dark strip sets total.

3. From *each* strip set, cut:

- 4 of Small Triangle Pattern

4. Referring to Cut and Assemble A Blocks, Step 6, *page 113,* sew together two light small triangles and two dark small triangles to make a small C block. The block should be 6½" square including seam allowances. Repeat to make 80 small C blocks total.

Assemble Quilt Top

1. Referring to **Quilt Assembly Diagram,** lay out 32 large A and B blocks and 96 small A, B, and C blocks in sections. Make sure dark batiks in blocks are oriented at top and bottom.

2. Sew together pieces to make subsections (most subsections consist of a pair of small blocks sewn together, then joined to a large block). When joining pairs of small blocks, press seams in opposite directions, then sew pairs together.

Quilt Assembly Diagram

3. Join subsections into sections; where seams meet, press in opposite directions. Sew together sections in three vertical rows; leave seams at red dots partially open in order to add bottom horizontal section. Add horizontal section and finish seams to complete quilt top. Press seams as necessary to make quilt top lie flat.

Finish Quilt

From violet-blue batik, cut:
- 10—2½×42" binding strips

1. Layer quilt top, batting, and backing; baste. (For details, see Complete Quilt, *page 159*.)

2. Quilt as desired. Mabeth machine-quilted an allover jagged spiral design across the quilt top **(Quilting Diagram).**

3. Bind with violet-blue batik binding strips. (For details, see Complete Quilt.)

Quilting Diagram

ME AND MY SHADOW

A subdued color palette still produces dramatic results.

Materials

⅜ yard brown tone-on-tone (binding)

6—18×22" pieces (fat quarters) *or* 1½ yards total assorted medium and dark prints in brown, dark gray, and teal (blocks)

6—18×22" pieces (fat quarters) *or* 1½ yards total assorted light prints in tan, cream, gray, and taupe (blocks)

1⅝ yards backing fabric

39×57" batting

Finished quilt: 30½×48½"

Cut Fabrics

Cut pieces in the order that follows in each section.

This project uses *Modern Mix* patterns on *Pattern Sheet 1.*

From brown tone-on-tone, cut:
- 4—2½×42" binding strips

Cut and Assemble A Blocks

The following instructions result in two large A blocks and one small A block. Repeat cutting and assembly steps to make six large A blocks and three small A blocks total.

From *each* of one medium or dark print and a light print, cut:
- 2—2⅝×22" strips

From *each* of a second medium or dark print and a light print, cut:
- 2—1¾×22" strips

From *each* of a third medium or dark print and a light print, cut:
- 2—1¼×22" strips

From *each* of a fourth medium or dark print and a light print, cut:
- 2—2½×22" strips

continued

1. Referring to Cut and Assemble A Blocks, Step 1, *page 112,* use medium or dark print 2⅝×22", 1¾×22", 1¼×22", and 2½×22" strips in desired order to make two identical dark strip sets.

2. Referring to Cut and Assemble A Blocks, Step 2, *page 113,* use light print 2⅝×22", 1¾×22", 1¼×22", and 2½×22" strips (arranged in the same strip-width order as the dark strip sets) to make two identical light strip sets.

3. Referring to **Diagram 3** on *page 113,* from *each* light and dark strip set, cut:

- 2 of Large Triangle Pattern
- 1 of Small Triangle Pattern

4. Referring to **Diagram 4** on *page 113,* lay out two matching dark large triangles and two matching light large triangles. Sew together large triangles in pairs; press seams toward dark triangles. Join pairs to make a large A block; press seam in one direction. The block should be 12½" square including seam allowances.

5. Repeat Step 4 with remaining large triangles to make a second large A block; it will have the opposite color progression of the first block.

6. Referring to Diagram 6, *page 113,* repeat Step 4 with small triangles to make a small A block. The block should be 6½" square including seam allowances.

Cut and Assemble C Blocks

1. From remaining assorted medium or dark print scraps and assorted light print scraps, cut:

- 22"-long strips in a variety of widths ranging from 1" to 2½"

2. Sew together enough medium or dark print strips to make a dark strip set at least 3⅝" wide. Press seams toward top strip. Repeat to make a coordinating light strip set with the same strip widths. Press seams toward bottom strip.

3. Repeat Step 2 to make seven pairs of light and dark strip sets total.

4. From *each* strip set, cut:

- 4 of Small Triangle Pattern

5. Referring to **Diagram 6** on *page 113,* sew together two matching light small triangles and two matching dark small triangles to make a small C block. The block should be 6½" square including seam allowances. Repeat to make 14 small C blocks.

Assemble Quilt Top

1. Referring to **Quilt Assembly Diagram**, lay out six large A blocks and 16 small A and C blocks in sections (you will have one small block left over). Make sure medium or dark prints in blocks are oriented at top and bottom.

2. Referring to Assemble Quilt Top, Step 2, *page 114,* sew together pieces to make subsections.

3. Join subsections into sections; where seams meet, press in opposite directions. Sew together sections in four horizontal rows to complete quilt top. Press seams as necessary to make quilt top lie flat.

Finish Quilt

1. Layer quilt top, batting, and backing; baste. (For details, see Complete Quilt, *page 159.*)

2. Quilt as desired. This quilt is stitched in the ditch with an X through each block.

3. Bind with brown tone-on-tone binding strips. (For details, see Complete Quilt.)

Quilt Assembly Diagram

RASPBERRY-LIMEADE TABLE TOPPER

You will be tickled pink with this charming nine-block treat.

Materials

1⅜ yards total assorted pink prints (blocks)

1⅜ yards total assorted green prints (blocks)

¾ yard white-and-pink polka dot (border)

½ yard pink floral (binding)

3 yards backing fabric

52" square batting

Finished quilt: 43½" square

continued

Assemble Blocks

1. Referring to Cut and Assemble A Blocks, Step 1, *page 112,* use a pink print 2⅝×36" strip, a green print 1¼×36" strip, a pink print 1¾×36" strip, and a green print 2½×36" strip to make a strip set **(Diagram 7).** Repeat to make four strip sets with different prints arranged in the same color and strip-width order.

2. Referring to **Diagram 7**, from *each* strip set, cut four of Large Triangle Pattern, yielding a total of eight triangles with pink print on base of triangle and eight triangles with green print on base.

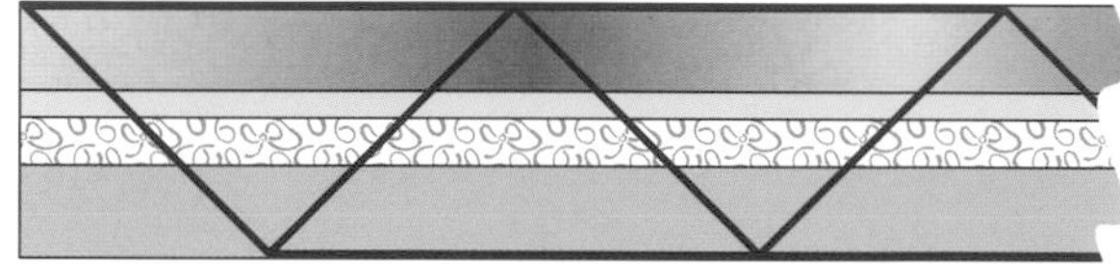

Diagram 7

3. Referring to **Diagram 8**, lay out two pairs of matching triangles with pink prints at the base, placing triangles with matching prints opposite each other. Sew together triangles in pairs. Press seams in opposite directions. Join pairs to make a pink block; press seam in one direction. The block should be 12½" square including seam allowances. (The block will have a narrow *green* strip forming a square.)

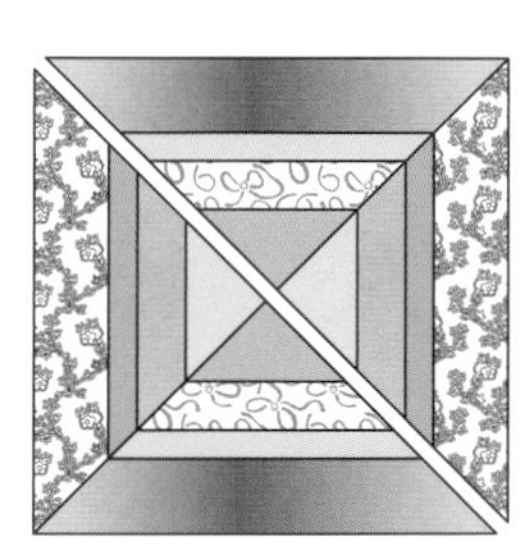

Diagram 8

4. Repeat Step 3 to make a second pink block. Using pairs of matching triangles with green prints at the base, repeat Step 3 to make two green blocks.

5. Referring to Cut and Assemble A Blocks, Step 1, *page 112,* use a green print 2⅝×36" strip, a pink print 1¼×36" strip, a green print 1¾×36" strip, and a pink print 2½×36" strip to make a strip set (colors will be the reverse of those shown in **Diagram 7**). Repeat to make six strip sets with different prints arranged in the same color and strip-width order.

6. From *each* strip set, cut four of Large Triangle Pattern, yielding a total of 12 triangles with pink print on base of triangle and 12 triangles with green print on base.

Cut Fabrics

Cut pieces in the following order.

This project uses *Modern Mix* Large Triangle Pattern on *Pattern Sheet 1.*

From assorted pink prints, cut:
- 4—2⅝×36" strips
- 6—2½×36" strips
- 4—1¾×36" strips
- 6—1¼×36" strips

From assorted green prints, cut:
- 6—2⅝×36" strips
- 4—2½×36" strips
- 6—1¾×36" strips
- 4—1¼×36" strips

From white-and-pink polka dot, cut:
- 5—4×42" strips for border

From pink floral, cut:
- 5—2½×42" binding strips

7. Referring to **Diagram 9**, repeat Step 3 to make a pink block. (The block will have a narrow *pink* strip forming a square.)

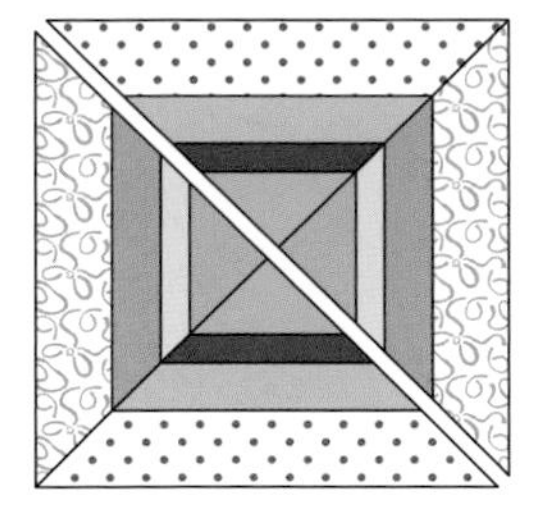
Diagram 9

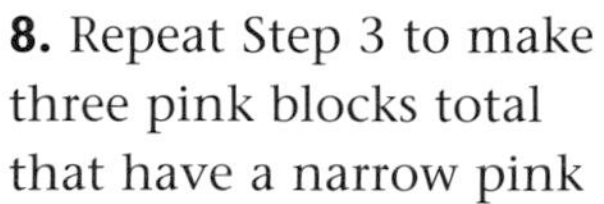

8. Repeat Step 3 to make three pink blocks total that have a narrow pink strip. Using pairs of matching triangles with green prints at the base, repeat Step 3 to make three green blocks that have a narrow pink strip.

Assemble Quilt Top

1. Referring to **Quilt Assembly Diagram**, lay out all blocks in three rows, alternating pink and green blocks. (You will have one green block left over.)

2. Sew together blocks in each row. Press seams in one direction, alternating direction with each row.

3. Join rows to make quilt center; press seams in one direction. The quilt center should be 36½" square including seam allowances.

Add Border

1. Cut and piece white-and-pink polka dot 4×42" strips to make:

- 2—4×43½" border strips
- 2—4×36½" border strips

2. Sew short border strips to opposite edges of quilt center. Add long border strips to remaining edges to complete quilt top. Press all seams toward border.

Finish Quilt

1. Layer quilt top, batting, and backing; baste. (For details, see Complete Quilt, *page 159*.) Quilt as desired.

2. Bind with pink floral binding strips. (For details, see Complete Quilt.)

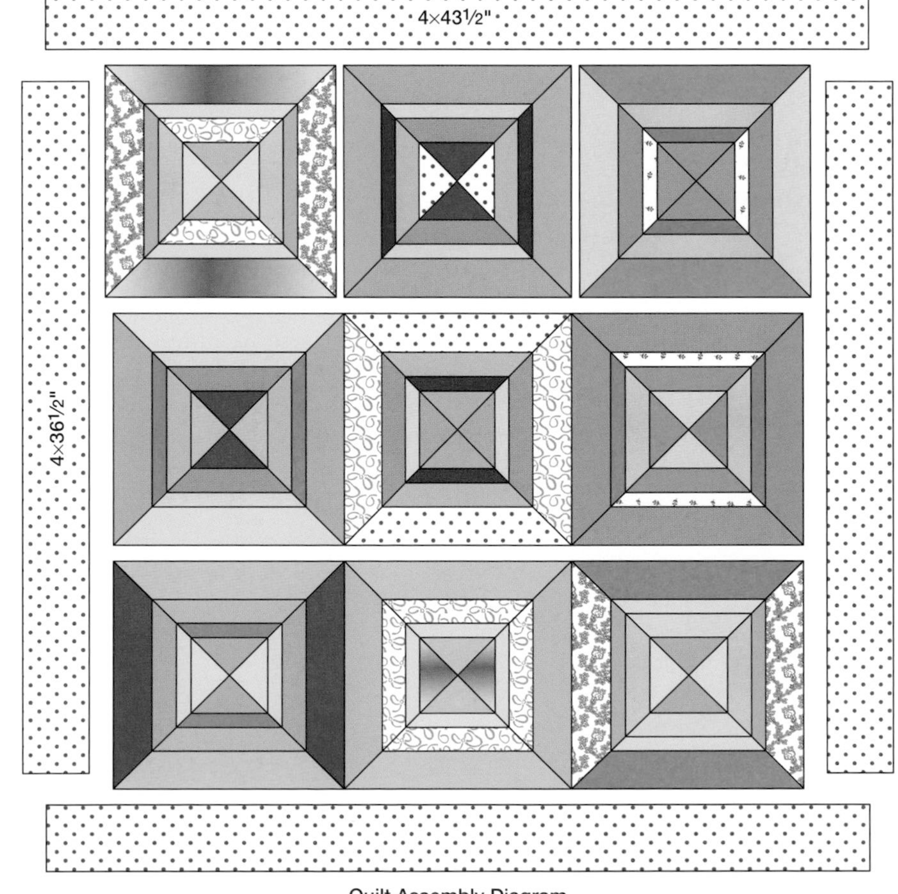

Quilt Assembly Diagram

RHYTHM & *Blues*

Think the blocks in this quilt are set diagonally? Take a closer look and you'll discover two simple blocks designer Monique Dillard straight-set in a cleverly planned color arrangement.

Materials

2⅔ yards total *or* 13—18×22" pieces (fat quarters) assorted cream-and-blue prints (blocks)

1⅔ yards total *or* 8—18×22" pieces (fat quarters) assorted dark blue prints (blocks)

⅓ yard cream print (inner border)

1⅞ yards navy blue print (outer border, binding)

4 yards backing fabric

70×79" batting

Finished quilt: 62×71"
Finished blocks: 4½" square

Quantities are for 44/45"-wide, 100% cotton fabrics. **Measurements** include ¼" seam allowances. Sew with right sides together unless otherwise stated.

Cut Fabrics

Cut pieces in the following order.

If you're working with fat quarters, see Tips for Cutting Fat Quarters, *page 122,* to determine how many pieces you'll need to cut from each one.

From assorted cream-and-blue prints, cut:
- 39—2×21" strips
- 19—5¾" squares, cutting each diagonally twice in an X for 76 triangles total
- 26—5" squares

From assorted dark blue prints, cut:
- 49—5¾" squares, cutting each diagonally twice in an X for 196 triangles total

From cream print, cut:
- 6—1½×42" strips for inner border

From navy blue print, cut:
- 7—5½×42" strips for outer border
- 7—2½×42" binding strips

Assemble Rail Fence Blocks

1. Sew together three assorted cream-and-blue print 2×21" strips to make a strip set **(Diagram 1)**. Press seams in one direction. Repeat to make 13 strip sets total.

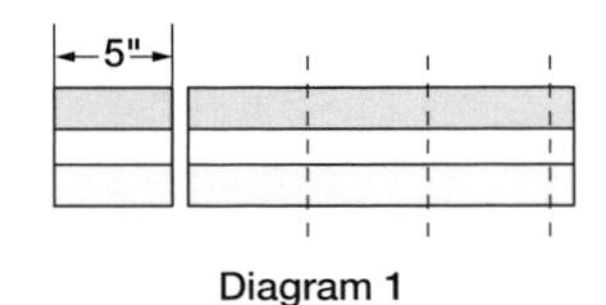

Diagram 1

2. Cut strip sets into 49—5"-wide Rail Fence blocks **(Diagram 1)**. Each block should be 5" square including seam allowances.

continued

Plan Quilt Layout and Assemble Hourglass Blocks

Designer Monique Dillard carefully planned her hourglass blocks so that four matching dark blue print triangles would surround each Rail Fence block. To replicate the look, lay out quilt center blocks, squares, and triangles prior to assembling hourglass blocks. For a less-planned look, skip steps 1–3 and make hourglass blocks as indicated in steps 4–7.

1. Referring to **Quilt Assembly Diagram** and **Diagram 2,** lay out assorted cream-and-blue print 5" squares and Rail Fence blocks in 13 rows on a design wall or other large surface, leaving 5" squares of space for hourglass blocks to be placed later.

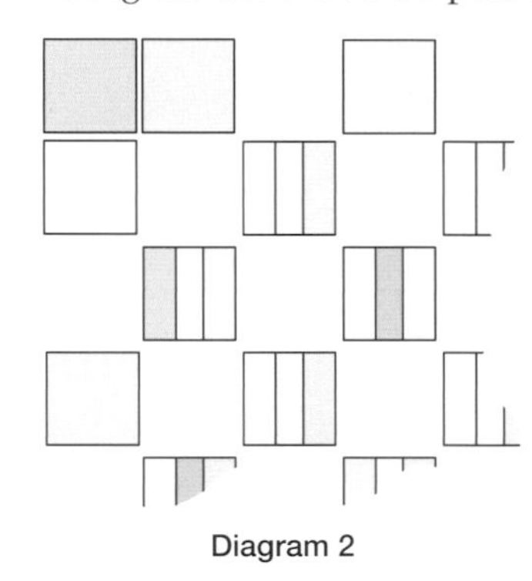
Diagram 2

2. Referring to **Quilt Assembly Diagram** and **Diagram 3,** position four matching dark blue print triangles around each Rail Fence block.

3. Referring to **Quilt Assembly Diagram** and **Diagram 4,** fill in all empty areas with assorted cream-and-blue print triangles.

Diagram 3

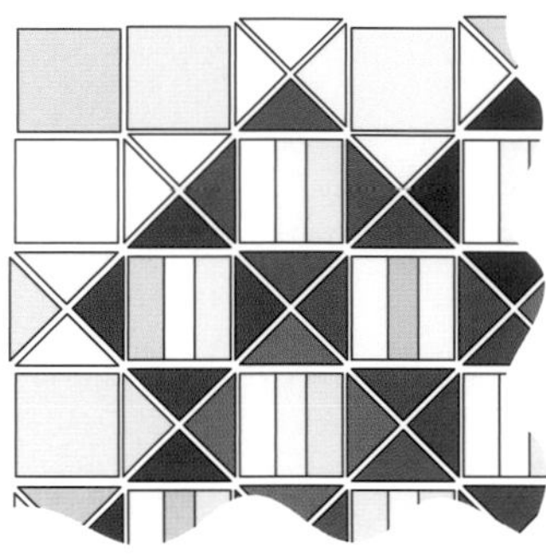
Diagram 4

4. Referring to **Diagram 5,** remove a group of four dark blue print triangles from design wall. Sew together triangles in pairs. Press seams in opposite directions. Join pairs to make hourglass block A. Press seam in one direction. The block should be 5" square including seam allowances. Return the block to its original place on design wall. Repeat to make 32 total of hourglass block A.

Diagram 5
Block A

Tips for Cutting Fat Quarters

If you are using fat quarters for *Rhythm & Blues,* cut the following pieces:

From *each* of 6 cream-and-blue fat quarters, cut:
- 3—2×21" strips
- 2—5¾" squares, cutting each diagonally twice in an X for eight triangles total
- 2—5" squares

From *each* of 7 remaining cream-and-blue fat quarters, cut:
- 3—2×21" strips
- 1—5¾" square, cutting diagonally twice in an X for four triangles total
- 2—5" squares

From one dark blue fat quarter, cut:
- 7—5¾" squares, cutting each diagonally twice in an X for 28 triangles total

From *each* of the seven remaining dark blue fat quarters, cut:
- 6—5¾" squares, cutting each diagonally twice in an X for 24 triangles total

5. Referring to **Diagram 6**, remove a group of three dark blue print triangles and one cream-and-blue print triangle; repeat Step 4 assembly instructions to make hourglass block B. Repeat to make 14 total of hourglass block B.

Diagram 6
Block B

6. Referring to **Diagram 7**, remove a group of two dark blue print triangles and two cream-and-blue print triangles; repeat Step 4 assembly instructions to make hourglass block C. Repeat to make four total of hourglass block C.

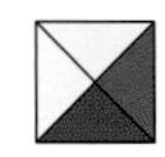

Diagram 7
Block C

7. Referring to **Diagram 8**, remove a group of one dark blue print triangle and three cream-and-blue print triangles; repeat Step 4 assembly instructions to make hourglass block D. Repeat to make 18 total of hourglass block D.

Diagram 8
Block D

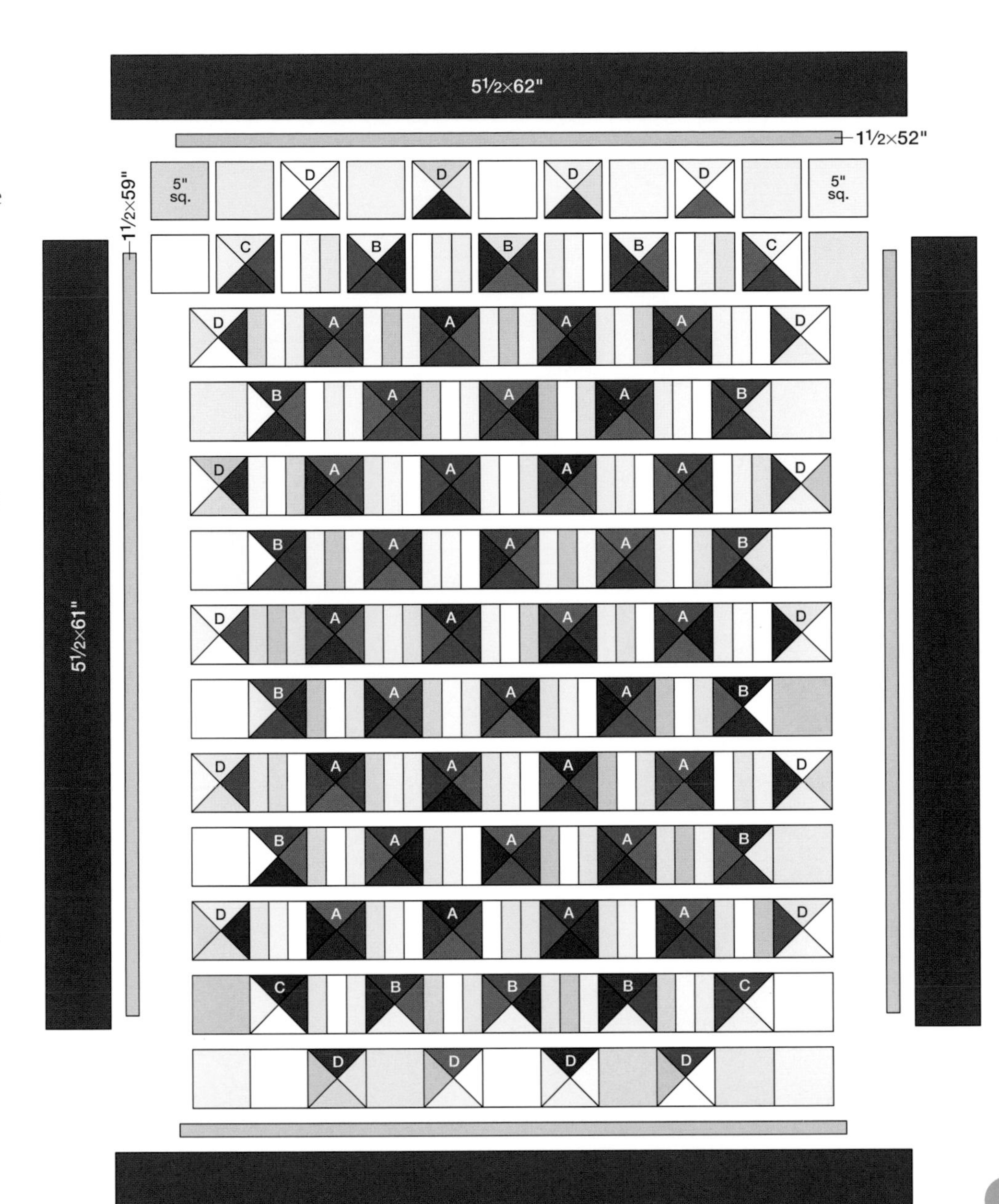

Quilt Assembly Diagram

Assemble Quilt Top

1. Referring to **Quilt Assembly Diagram**, sew together pieces in each row. Press seams toward Rail Fence blocks and 5" squares.

2. Join rows to make quilt center. Press seams in one direction. The quilt center should be 50×59" including seam allowances.

3. Cut and piece cream print 1½×42" strips to make:

- 2—1½×59" inner border strips
- 2—1½×52" inner border strips

4. Sew long inner border strips to long edges of quilt center. Add short inner border strips to remaining edges. Press all seams toward inner border.

5. Cut and piece navy blue print 5½×42" strips to make:

- 2—5½×62" outer border strips
- 2—5½×61" outer border strips

6. Sew 5½×61" outer border strips to long edges of quilt center. Add 5½×62" outer border strips to remaining edges to complete quilt top. Press all seams toward outer border.

continued

Finish Quilt

1. Layer quilt top, batting, and backing; baste. (For details, see Complete Quilt, *page 159*.)

2. Quilt as desired. Sue Glorch machine-quilted a flower motif in each Rail Fence block and a curved triangle in each dark blue print triangle **(Quilting Diagram).** She quilted a feather design in the remaining triangles, squares, and outer border.

3. Bind with navy blue print binding strips. (For details, see Complete Quilt.)

Quilting Diagram

optional colors

Memory Lane

Quilt tester Laura Boehnke gave this new quilt old-fashioned appeal by combining 1930s prints in light and medium values to make a wall hanging version of *Rhythm & Blues*.

"The light areas are great for showcasing quilting designs," Laura says.

FLANNEL KID'S QUILT

Use soft flannels to make an oh-so-cuddly quilt.

Materials

10—18×22" pieces (fat quarters) assorted flannels in blue, yellow, pink, green, and peach (blocks)

½ yard yellow flannel (binding)

3 yards backing fabric

54" square batting

Finished quilt: 45½" square

Cut Fabrics

From assorted flannels, cut:

- 75—2×21" strips

From yellow flannel, cut:

- 5—2½×42" binding strips

continued

Assemble Rail Fence Blocks

1. Referring to Assemble Rail Fence Blocks, Step 1, *page 121,* use three assorted flannel 2×21" strips to make a strip set. Repeat to make 25 strip sets total.

2. Referring to Assemble Rail Fence Blocks, Step 2, *page 121,* cut strip sets into 100—5"-wide Rail Fence blocks.

Assemble Quilt Top

Referring to photo, *below,* lay out Rail Fence blocks in 10 rows. Sew together blocks in each row. Press seams in one direction, alternating direction with each row. Join rows to complete quilt top. Press seams in one direction.

Finish Quilt

1. Layer quilt top, batting, and backing; baste. (For details, see Complete Quilt, *page 159.*)

2. Quilt as desired. Alternating swirls and wavy lines are machine-quilted in each block of the featured quilt.

3. Bind with yellow flannel binding strips. (For details, see Complete Quilt.)

FARMER'S MARKET TABLE MAT

Mix and match fruit and veggie prints for an easy-to-sew table mat.

Materials

24—6" squares assorted fruit and vegetable prints in red, orange, yellow, green, blue, purple, and tan (blocks)

1/3 yard blue print (binding)

3/4 yard backing fabric

27×36" batting

15—1/2"-diameter buttons: 3 *each* of red, yellow, green, blue, and purple

Finished quilt: 18 1/2×27 1/2"

Cut Fabrics

Cut pieces in the following order.

From assorted prints, cut:

- 24—5 3/4" squares, cutting each diagonally twice in an X for 96 triangles total

From blue print, cut:

- 3—2 1/2×42" binding strips

Assemble Hourglass Blocks

Referring to **Diagram 5**, *page 122*, and photo, *right,* lay out four assorted print triangles in pairs. Sew together triangles in each pair; press seams in opposite directions. Join pairs to make an hourglass block. Press seam in one direction. The block should be 5" square including seam allowances. Repeat to make 24 hourglass blocks total.

Assemble Quilt Top

Referring to photo, *above right,* lay out hourglass blocks in six rows. Sew together blocks in each row. Press seams in one direction, alternating direction with each row. Join rows to complete quilt top; press seams in one direction.

Finish Quilt

1. Layer quilt top, batting, and backing; baste. (For details, see Complete Quilt, *page 159.*)

2. Quilt as desired. Referring to photo, *above,* hand-sew a button at each block intersection.

3. Bind with blue print binding strips. (For details, see Complete Quilt.)

148

138

130

140

APPLIQUÉ YOUR WAY

Appliqué has been transformed by today's tools and techniques. You can choose from traditional hand- or machine-stitched patterns, fusible-web motifs, or dimensional designs. Experiment and expand your appliquéing repertoire by trying myriad techniques in this chapter. Or choose the method that you enjoy most, then adapt the pattern to fit your favorite style.

BUDDING *Beauty*

A soft butter yellow teamed with solid white in this bed-size quilt by designer Linda Hohag provides the perfect background for the bright '30s print appliqués.

Materials

1½ yards total assorted 1930s prints (bud appliqués)

⅓ yard solid green (stem appliqués)

4½ yards solid white (appliqué foundations, blocks)

2½ yards solid yellow (blocks, inner border)

1⅛ yards yellow print (blocks)

1⅝ yards green print (middle border, binding)

2¾ yards blue print (outer border)

8⅛ yards backing fabric

97×112" batting

Heat-resistant template plastic

Liquid or spray starch

Clear monofilament thread

Finished quilt: 88¼×103¾"
Finished blocks: 11" square

Quantities are for 44/45"-wide, 100% cotton fabrics. **Measurements** include ¼" seam allowances. Sew with right sides together unless otherwise stated.

SIZE OPTIONS: For a chart of optional sizes, turn to *Pattern Sheet 2*.

Cut Fabrics

Cut pieces in the following order. Cut inner and outer border strips lengthwise (parallel to the selvages).

The Bud Pattern is on *Pattern Sheet 1*. Designer Linda Hohag uses a template-plastic-and-starch method for appliquéing; for instructions, see Prepare Bud Appliqués, *page 132*.

From assorted 1930s prints, cut:
- 320 of Bud Pattern

From solid green, cut:
- 80—¾×4" strips

From solid white, cut:
- 20—12" squares
- 5—9" squares, cutting each diagonally twice in an X for 20 large triangles total (you will use 18)
- 60—4¾" squares, cutting each in half diagonally for 120 small triangles total

From solid yellow, cut:
- 2—1½×85¾" inner border strips
- 2—1½×72¼" inner border strips
- 49—6⅜" squares, cutting each in half diagonally for 98 large triangles total

From yellow print, cut:
- 30—6" squares

From green print, cut:
- 9—2½×42" strips for middle border
- 10—2½×42" binding strips

From blue print, cut:
- 2—6½×91¾" outer border strips
- 2—6½×88¼" outer border strips

continued

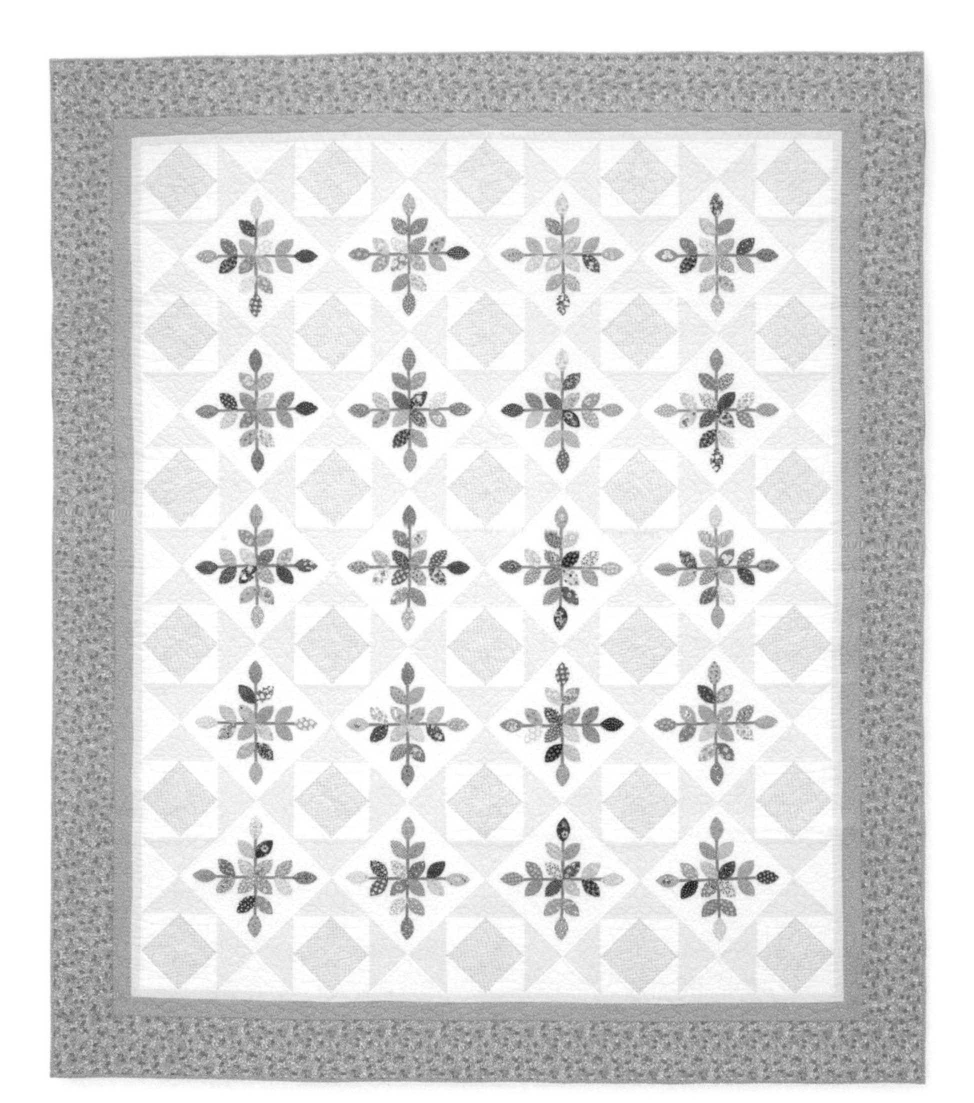

Prepare Bud Appliqués

1. Place heat-resistant template plastic over Bud Pattern. Using a pencil, trace pattern onto plastic **(Diagram 1)**. Cut out on drawn lines to make a bud template.

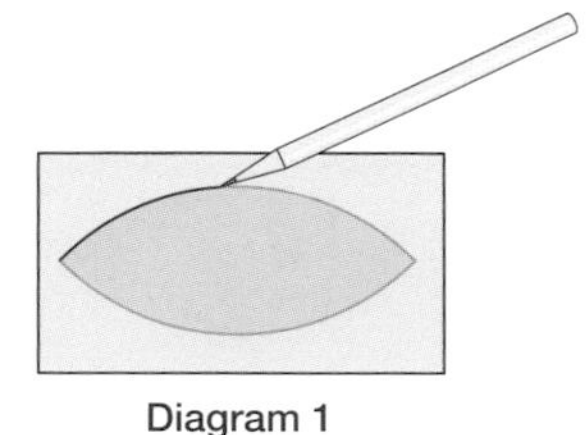

Diagram 1

2. Place bud template on wrong side of a 1930s print fabric. Cut out bud appliqué piece, adding a ¼" seam allowance to edges **(Diagram 2)**. If desired, trim across points to reduce bulk.

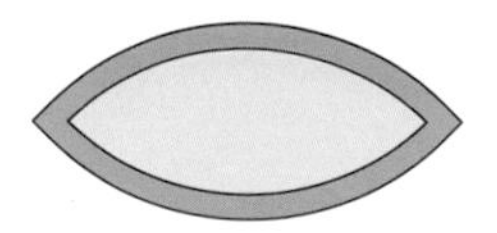

Diagram 2

3. Spray or pour a small amount of starch into a dish. Place template-topped fabric on a pressing surface covered with a tea towel or muslin. Dip a cotton swab in starch and moisten seam allowance of appliqué piece **(Diagram 3)**.

Diagram 3

4. Use tip of a hot dry iron to turn seam allowance over edge of template; press until fabric is dry **(Diagram 4)**. Press entire seam allowance, adding starch as necessary and ensuring fabric is pressed taut against template. (To make sharp points on bud appliqué, see Tip, *opposite*.)

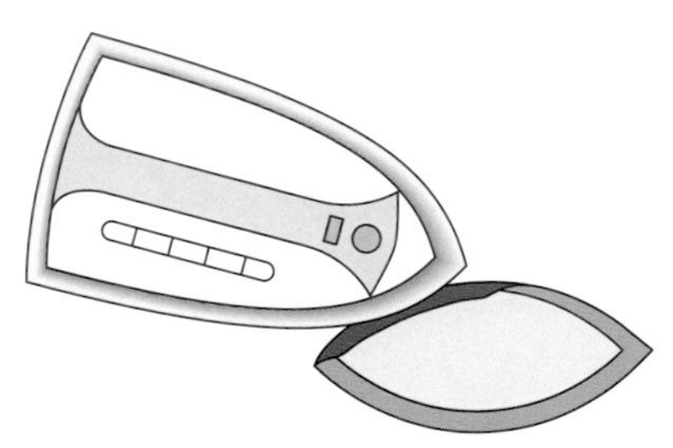

Diagram 4

5. Turn over template and appliqué piece. Press appliqué from right side, then remove template to make a bud appliqué.

6. Repeat steps 2–5 to make 320 bud appliqués total.

Prepare Stem Appliqués

Turn under a scant ¼" on each long edge of a solid green ¾×4" strip. Press, starching if desired, to make a stem appliqué. Repeat to make 80 stem appliqués total.

Appliqué Blocks

1. Fold a solid white 12" square in half diagonally twice. Lightly finger-press each fold to create a foundation square with appliqué placement guidelines; unfold.

2. Referring to **Appliqué Placement Diagram,** lay out four stem appliqués and 16 bud appliqués on foundation square; pin or glue-baste in place.

Appliqué Placement Diagram

3. Using clear monofilament thread and working from bottom layer to top, machine-zigzag-stitch around each appliqué to make an appliquéd block.

4. Soak appliquéd block in cold water to remove starch. Machine-dry with dry towel to help absorb excess water. Trim excess foundation fabric from behind appliqués, leaving ¼" seam allowances. Press block from wrong side and trim to 11½" square including seam allowances.

5. Repeat steps 1–4 to make 20 appliquéd blocks total.

Assemble Square-in-a-Square Blocks and Units

1. Sew solid white small triangles to opposite edges of a yellow print 6" square **(Diagram 5).** Add solid white small triangles to remaining edges to make a Square-in-a-Square unit. Press all seams toward triangles. The unit should be 8¼" square including seam allowances. Repeat to make 30 Square-in-a-Square units total.

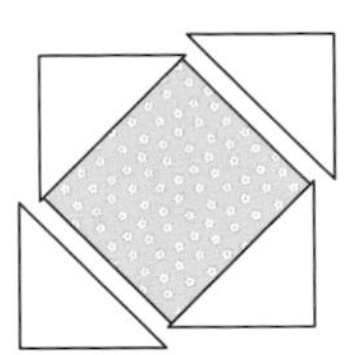

Diagram 5

2. Sew solid yellow large triangles to opposite edges of a Square-in-a-Square unit. Add solid yellow large triangles to remaining edges to make a Square-in-a-Square block **(Diagram 6).** Press all seams toward solid yellow triangles. The block should be 11½" square including seam allowances. Repeat to make 12 Square-in-a-Square blocks total.

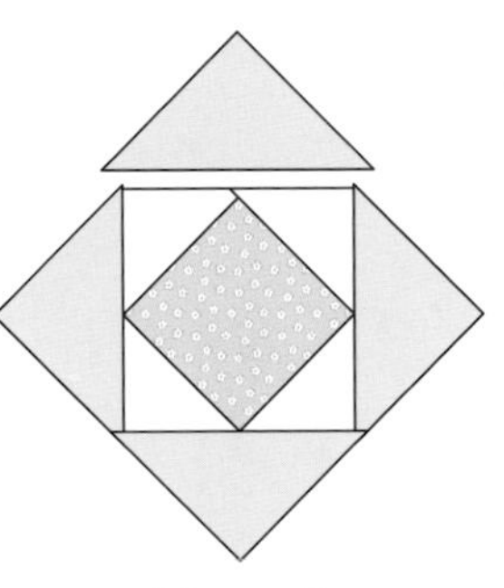

Diagram 6

3. Sew solid yellow large triangles to opposite edges of a Square-in-a-Square unit. Add a solid yellow large triangle to one remaining edge to make a side unit **(Diagram 7).** Press all seams toward solid yellow triangles. Repeat to make 14 side units total.

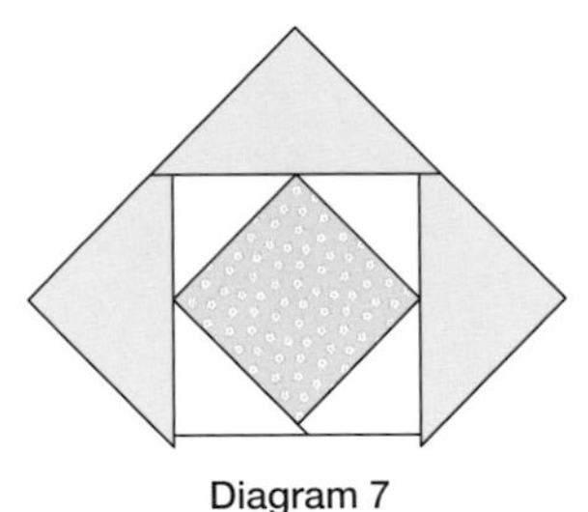

Diagram 7

continued

TIP: *To make a sharp point on each end of bud appliqué, moisten the seam allowance with starch and fold the fabric point straight back over the point of the template; press. Push an adjacent edge of the seam allowance over the template edge and press. Repeat with remaining adjacent seam allowance.*

4. Join two solid white large triangles and two solid yellow large triangles to make mirror-image triangle pairs **(Diagram 8).** Press seams toward solid yellow triangles. Join triangle pairs to adjacent edges of a Square-in-a-Square unit to make a corner unit. Press seams toward triangle pairs. Repeat to make four corner units total.

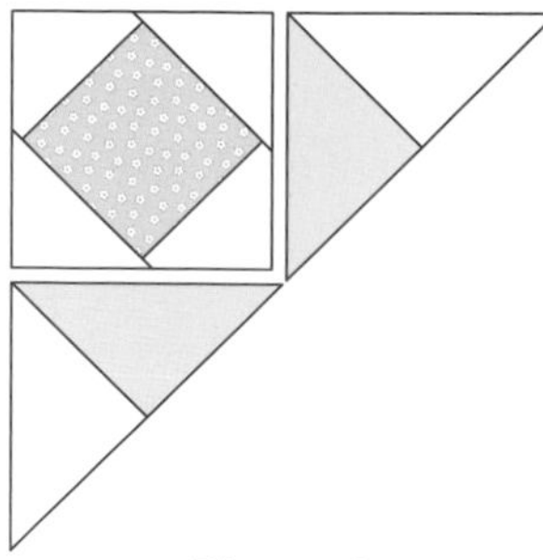

Diagram 8

Assemble Quilt Center

1. Referring to **Quilt Assembly Diagram,** lay out appliquéd blocks, Square-in-a-Square blocks, side units, and 10 solid white large triangles in diagonal rows.

2. Sew together pieces in each row. Press seams toward Square-in-a-Square blocks and side units. Join rows; press seams in one direction.

Quilt Assembly Diagram

3. Add a corner unit to each corner to make quilt center; press seams toward corner units. The quilt center should be 70¼×85¾" including seam allowances.

Add Borders

1. Sew long solid yellow inner border strips to long edges of quilt center. Join short solid yellow inner border strips to remaining edges. Press all seams toward inner border.

2. Cut and piece green print 2½×42" strips to make:
- 2—2½×87¾" middle border strips
- 2—2½×76¼" middle border strips

3. Sew long middle border strips to long edges of quilt center. Join short middle border strips to remaining edges. Press all seams toward middle border.

4. Sew long blue print outer border strips to long edges of quilt center. Join short blue print outer border strips to remaining edges to complete quilt top. Press all seams toward outer border.

Finish Quilt

1. Layer quilt top, batting, and backing; baste. (For details, see Complete Quilt, *page 159*.)

2. Quilt as desired. Machine-quilter Jenise Antony stitched a floral design in each Square-in-a-Square unit and a second floral design in each solid yellow and solid white large triangle **(Quilting Diagram).** She stippled the background of each appliquéd block and stitched in the ditch of each border. She quilted a continuous chain in the middle border and a feather design in the outer border.

Quilting Diagram

3. Bind with green print binding strips. (For details, see Complete Quilt.)

optional colors

Northern View

Complete with canoes, moose, and bears, quilt tester Laura Boehnke took *Budding Beauty* up north using woodland-inspired prints. To highlight the star pattern formed when four partial Square-in-a-Square blocks surround one appliquéd block, she chose a richly colored leaf print. With fusible appliqué and machine blanket stitching, Laura quickly transformed the bud and stem appliqués into leaves and branches, picking up purples, tans, greens, and browns of the coordinating prints. She eliminated the wide outer border to finish with a 29¾"-square wall hanging.

SUNFLOWER TABLE RUNNER

Layers of felted wool and buttons add dimension to an inviting folk art accent.

Materials

18×22" piece (fat quarter) gold felted wool (petals)

12×43" rectangle green felted wool (appliqué foundation)

13×44" rectangle brown felted wool (backing)

14—½"-diameter assorted vintage buttons: brown

2—¾"-diameter assorted vintage buttons: brown

Perle cotton No. 3: light brown

Embroidery needle

Finished table runner: 13×44"

Cut Fabrics

Cut pieces in the following order. This project uses *Budding Beauty* Bud Pattern on *Pattern Sheet 1* to create the petals. To make a template of the pattern, see Make and Use Templates, *page 157;* do not add a seam allowance when cutting wool petals.

To felt wool, machine-wash it in a hot-water-wash, cold-rinse cycle with a small amount of detergent. Machine-dry on high heat; steam-press.

From gold wool, cut:

- 48 of Bud Pattern for petals

Appliqué Petals

1. Referring to upper section of **Appliqué Placement Diagram**, position eight gold wool petals on one end of green wool 12×43" rectangle; pin. Using thread that matches petals, secure pieces with tiny tack stitches, leaving ends of petals loose.

2. Position and pin another layer of eight petals atop Step 1 pieces, offsetting petals (**Appliqué Placement Diagram**, lower section). Tack-stitch in place.

3. Referring to photo, *right,* tack-stitch a third layer of eight petals to Step 2 pieces. Push loose ends of third layer of petals slightly toward center of flower to create a "bump" on each petal. Hand-stitch petal ends in place.

4. Referring to photo, *opposite,* hand-stitch seven ½"-diameter buttons and a ¾"-diameter button over center of petals to make sunflower.

5. Using remaining gold wool petals and buttons, repeat steps 1–4 on opposite end of green wool rectangle to make table runner top.

Finish Table Runner

1. Center table runner top over brown wool 13×44" backing rectangle; pin or baste layers together.

2. Using light brown perle cotton and an embroidery needle, hand-stitch table runner top to backing with long running stitches to complete table runner.

Appliqué Placement Diagram

BLOOMING PINCUSHION

Use fusible and dimensional appliqué techniques to add texture.

Materials

18×22" piece (fat quarter) red print (appliqués)

7×15" rectangle green batik (pincushion)

Lightweight fusible web

Clear monofilament thread

1"-diameter button: red

1½ cups crushed walnut shells *or* other pincushion filler

Finished pincushion: 6" square

Cut Fabrics

Cut pieces in the order that follows in each section. This project uses *Budding Beauty* Bud Pattern on *Pattern Sheet 1* to create the petals.

The pincushion is made using dimensional and fusible-web appliqué methods. To cut and prepare the upper petals, see Prepare Dimensional Petals, *opposite*.

To use fusible web for appliquéing the lower petals, complete the following steps.

1. Lay fusible web, paper side up, over Bud Pattern. Use a pencil to trace the pattern six times, leaving ½" between tracings. Cut out each fusible-web petal shape roughly ¼" outside traced lines.

2. Following manufacturer's instructions, press each fusible-web petal shape onto wrong side of red print; let cool. Cut out fabric shapes on drawn lines. Peel off paper backings.

From red print, cut:
- 6 of Bud Pattern for fusible appliqué

From green batik, cut:
- 2—6½" squares

Appliqué Fusible Petals

1. Referring to **Appliqué Placement Diagram**, position six prepared petals on a green batik 6½" square. Fuse all pieces in place following manufacturer's directions.

Appliqué Placement Diagram

2. Using monofilament thread, machine-zigzag-stitch around each petal to make appliquéd foundation.

Prepare Dimensional Petals

To make a template of Bud Pattern, see Make and Use templates, *page 157*. Add a ¼" seam allowance when cutting out fabric shapes.

From red print, cut:
- 12 of Bud Pattern for dimensional appliqué

1. Layer two red print bud pieces right sides together. Sew around pair with ¼" seam allowance, leaving one end open **(Diagram 9)**. Trim seam allowance to ⅛" to make a dimensional petal. Turn petal right side out; press.

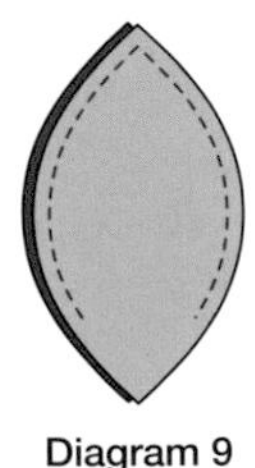

Diagram 9

Diagram 10

2. Make a small pleat in bottom of dimensional petal; tack pleat in place **(Diagram 10)**.

3. Repeat steps 1 and 2 to make six dimensional petals total.

Appliqué Dimensional Petals

1. Referring to **Diagram 11**, sew dimensional petals together, overlapping at base, to form a dimensional flower. Make several hand stitches on back of flower to secure petals.

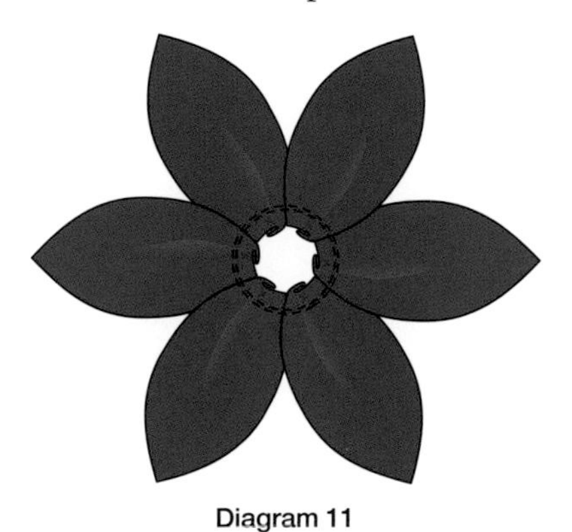

Diagram 11

2. Referring to photo, *below*, position dimensional flower on appliquéd foundation; secure flower with several stitches. Hand-sew red button to center of flower to make pincushion top.

Finish Pincushion

1. With right sides together, sew together pincushion top and remaining green batik 6½" square, leaving a 2" opening for turning. Trim corners.

2. Turn right side out. Fill with crushed walnut shells or desired filler. Whipstitch opening closed to complete pincushion.

Birds of a *Feather*

Build a fanciful quilt block by block, stitching either one mother bird or two baby birds in each. The curvy pieces are a snap to machine-appliqué, and the retro-inspired motif by designer Kevin Kosbab encourages the use of bold, bright fabrics.

Materials

¾ yard total assorted bright prints in blue, green, red, orange, and yellow (bird body and wing appliqués)

¾ yard total assorted bright solids in blue, green, red, orange, and yellow (bird body and wing appliqués)

⅛ yard solid orange (beak and feet appliqués)

1⅔ yards solid turquoise (appliqué foundations)

½ yard multicolor stripe (binding)

2½ yards backing fabric

45×54" batting

Freezer paper

Spray starch

Lightweight fusible web

Clear monofilament polyester or nylon thread

Finished quilt: 36½×45½"
Finished blocks: 9" square

Quantities are for 44/45"-wide, 100% cotton fabrics. **Measurements** include ¼" seam allowances. Sew with right sides together unless otherwise stated.

Cut Fabrics

Cut pieces in the following order. Patterns are on *Pattern Sheet 1.*

To make templates and prepare appliqué pieces A, B, E, and F, see Prepare Freezer-Paper Appliqués, *page 142.* To prepare appliqué pieces C, D, G, and H, see Prepare Fusible-Web Appliqués, *page 142.*

From assorted bright prints, cut:
- 1 of Pattern A
- 2 of Pattern A reversed
- 9 of Pattern E
- 6 of Pattern E reversed
- 2 of Pattern B
- 15 of Pattern F

From assorted bright solids, cut:
- 2 of Pattern A
- 9 of Pattern E
- 6 of Pattern E reversed
- 3 of Pattern B
- 15 of Pattern F

From solid orange, cut:
- 5 *each* of patterns C and D
- 30 *each* of patterns G and H

continued

Wee Wagon
AMF

From solid turquoise, cut:
• 20—9½" squares
From multicolor stripe, cut:
• 5—2½×42" binding strips

Prepare Freezer-Paper Appliqués

Designer Kevin Kosbab and quiltmaker Heather Kosbab, a son-mother team, used a freezer-paper-and-starch method for appliquéing the body (A and E) and wing (B and F) shapes. Instructions that follow are for this technique.

1. Lay freezer paper, shiny side down, over patterns A, A reversed, B, E, E reversed, and F. Use a pencil to trace each pattern the number of times indicated in cutting instructions, leaving ½" between tracings.

2. Place each sheet of drawn shapes, shiny side down, on a second sheet of freezer paper, also shiny side down. Fuse together with a hot dry iron. Cut out layered shapes on drawn lines to make freezer-paper templates.

3. Using a hot dry iron, press a freezer-paper template, shiny side down, onto wrong side of designated fabric; let cool. Cut out fabric shape, adding a scant ¼" seam allowance to all edges **(Diagram 1)**.

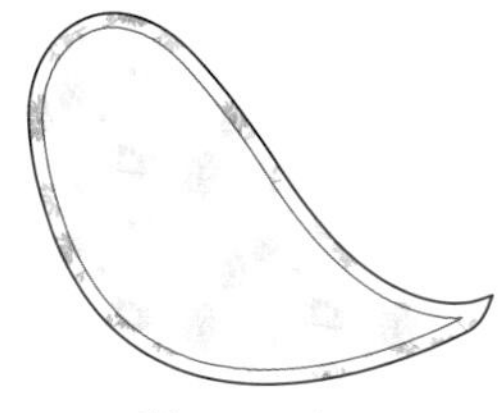

Diagram 1

4. Spray a small amount of starch into a dish or the cap of the starch bottle. Place a template-topped fabric shape on a pressing surface that is covered with a tea towel or muslin. Dip a small paintbrush or cotton swab into starch and moisten seam allowance of fabric shape **(Diagram 2)**.

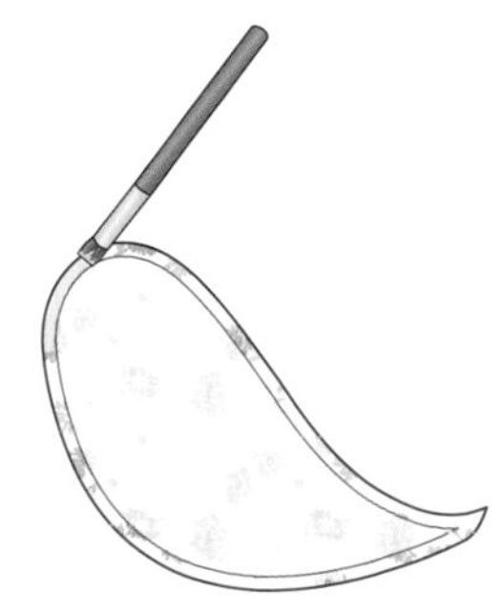

Diagram 2

5. Using tip of hot dry iron, turn seam allowance over edge of freezer-paper template; press until fabric is dry. Press entire seam allowance, adding starch as necessary and ensuring fabric is pressed taut against template. At each point, fold fabric point over template point, then turn adjacent edges. Carefully peel off template to prepare appliqué shape.

6. Repeat steps 3–5 to prepare remaining bird body and wing appliqués using fabrics indicated in cutting instructions.

Prepare Fusible-Web Appliqués

To use fusible web for appliquéing feet (C and G) and beak (D and H) shapes, complete the following steps.

1. Lay fusible web, paper side up, over patterns C, D, G, and H. Use a pencil to trace each pattern the number of times indicated in cutting instructions, leaving ½" between tracings. Cut out each fusible-web shape roughly ¼" outside traced lines.

2. Following manufacturer's instructions, press fusible-web shapes onto wrong side of solid orange fabric; let cool. Cut out fabric shapes on drawn lines. Peel off paper backings to prepare appliqués.

Appliqué Blocks

1. Referring to **Diagram 3**, position a bright print A body and solid orange C feet on a solid turquoise 9½" square. Pin feet in place; remove body appliqué.

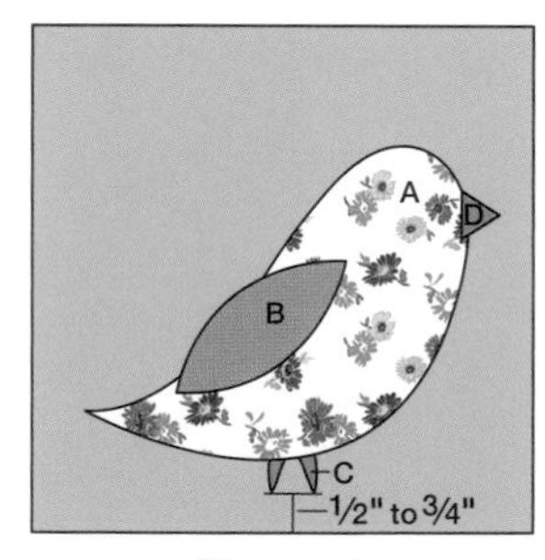

Diagram 3

2. Following manufacturer's directions, fuse feet in place. With orange thread and a short, narrow zigzag stitch, machine-appliqué feet (see Tip, *opposite*).

3. Reposition A body on solid turquoise square; pin. With clear monofilament thread and a blind-hem stitch, machine-appliqué body; to conceal backstitches, start and stop stitching where wing will overlap bird body. Referring to **Diagram 3**, position a bright solid B wing on bird body; pin and stitch in place.

4. Referring to Step 2, position, fuse, and stitch a solid orange D beak to complete a mother bird A block.

5. Using bright solid A bird bodies and bright print B wings, repeat steps 1–4 to make three mother bird A blocks total.

6. Position a bright print A reversed body, bright solid B wing, solid orange C feet, and solid orange D beak on a solid turquoise 9½" square in a mirror image of **Diagram 3.** Appliqué all pieces in place as before to make a mother bird B block. Repeat to make a second mother bird B block.

7. Referring to **Diagram 4**, position two E bodies (one solid and one print), two F wings (one solid and one print), two solid orange G feet, and two solid orange H beaks on a solid turquoise 9½" square. Appliqué pieces as before to make a baby bird A block. Repeat to make nine baby bird A blocks total.

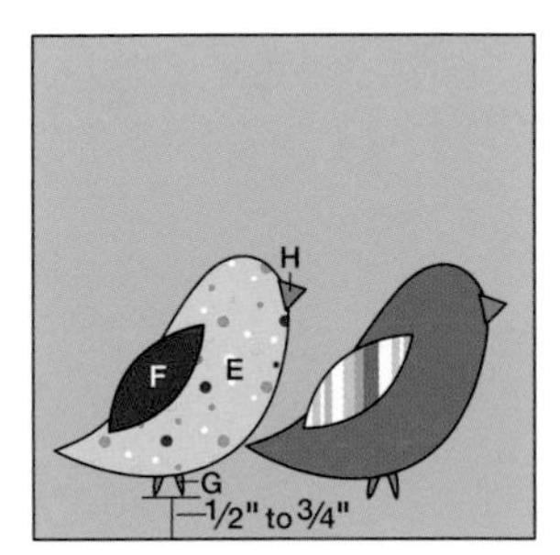

Diagram 4

8. Position two E reversed bodies (one solid and one print), two F wings (one solid and one print), two solid orange G feet, and two solid orange H beaks on a solid turquoise 9½" square in a mirror image of **Diagram 4.** Appliqué all pieces as before to make a baby bird B block. Repeat to make six baby bird B blocks total.

9. Using black thread, machine-satin-stitch an eye on each bird (see photo on *page 141*). Start with a narrow stitch, increase width, then narrow it again to make the eye round.

Assemble Quilt Top

1. Referring to **Quilt Assembly Diagram** for placement, lay out blocks in five rows. Sew together blocks in each row. Press seams in one direction, alternating direction with each row.

Quilt Assembly Diagram

TIP: *To avoid constantly changing thread and machine settings when making* Birds of a Feather, *designer Kevin Kosbab suggests laying out all appliqué shapes on the foundation squares. Appliqué all feet, then all bodies, all wings, and lastly, all beaks.*

continued

2. Join rows to complete quilt top. Press seams in one direction.

Finish Quilt

1. Layer quilt top, batting, and backing; baste. (For details, see Complete Quilt, *page 159*.)

2. Quilt as desired. To mimic feathers, Heather machine-quilted the solid turquoise background with a free-form shell design and stitched just outside the bird bodies and wings to make them stand out **(Quilting Diagram).**

3. Bind with multicolor stripe binding strips. (For details, see Complete Quilt.)

Quilting Diagram

ALL IN THE FAMILY PILLOW

Personalize a pillow with the number of feathered friends that fits your family.

Materials

7×9" piece *each* of felted wool in dark aqua plaid and light purple plaid (large bird body appliqués)

3×5" piece *each* of felted wool in light aqua plaid and dark purple plaid (large wing appliqués)

6" square gold felted wool (beak and feet appliqués)

6" square *each* of felted wool in light green herringbone, light purple herringbone, and light aqua houndstooth (small bird body appliqués)

2×4" piece *each* of felted wool in dark green herringbone, dark purple herringbone, and dark aqua houndstooth (small wing appliqués)

¾ yard brown linen (pillow top, backing)

Embroidery floss: aqua, purple, gold, and green to match appliqués

5 small beads: brown (bird eyes)

26"-long piece bead-and-felt trim: brown

4"-long piece sequin trim: purple

76"-long piece pleated ribbon trim: brown

12×24" pillow form *or* polyester fiberfill

Freezer paper

Fabric glue

Finished pillow: 24×12"

Cut Fabrics

Cut pieces in the following order. This project uses *Birds of a Feather* patterns on *Pattern Sheet 1*.

To felt wool, machine-wash it in a hot-water-wash, cold-rinse cycle. Machine-dry on high heat; steam-press.

To use freezer paper for cutting appliqué shapes, complete the following steps.

1. Lay freezer paper, shiny side down, over patterns. Use a pencil to trace each pattern the number of times indicated in cutting instructions, leaving ¼" between tracings. Cut out freezer-paper shapes roughly ⅛" outside drawn lines.

2. Using a hot dry iron, press each freezer-paper shape, shiny side down, onto right side of designated fabric; let cool. Cut out fabric shapes on drawn lines and peel off freezer paper. (Because felted wool does not fray, you do not need to add a seam allowance when cutting out appliqué shapes.)

From *each* dark aqua plaid wool and light purple plaid wool, cut:
- 1 of Pattern A

From *each* light aqua plaid wool and dark purple plaid wool, cut:
- 1 of Pattern B

From gold wool, cut:
- 2 *each* of patterns C and D
- 3 *each* of patterns G and H

Appliqué Placement Diagram

From *each* light green herringbone wool, light purple herringbone wool, and light aqua houndstooth wool, cut:
- 1 of Pattern E

From *each* dark green herringbone wool, dark purple herringbone wool, and dark aqua houndstooth wool, cut:
- 1 of Pattern F

From brown linen, cut:
- 1—14×26" rectangle
- 1—12½×24½" rectangle

Appliqué and Embellish Pillow Top

1. Referring to **Appliqué Placement Diagram,** position all wool appliqué shapes on brown linen 26×14" rectangle. Pin pieces in place.

2. Using two strands of matching embroidery floss, whipstitch pieces in place to make pillow top.

3. Trim pillow top to 24½×12½" including seam allowances.

4. Referring to photo, *opposite,* hand-sew a brown bead on each bird for eye.

continued

5. Referring to photo, *page 144,* hand-stitch brown bead-and-felt trim under bird appliqués.

6. Referring to photo, glue purple sequin trim on large purple bird for necklace.

Finish Pillow

1. Pin brown pleated ribbon trim to right side of pillow top, aligning trim with raw edges. Layer brown linen 24½×12½" backing rectangle over pillow top, right sides together. Sew together to make pillow cover, leaving an 8" opening along one long edge for turning.

2. Turn pillow cover right side out and insert pillow form or stuff with polyester fiberfill. Hand-stitch opening closed to complete pillow.

GRANDMA'S LITTLE BIRDIES

A small flock comes to roost on an endearing wall hanging.

Materials

3/8 yard multicolor print (bird body appliqué, binding)

1/2 yard total assorted bright prints in green, aqua, yellow, pink, and orange (bird body and wing appliqués)

1/8 yard yellow-and-orange print (beak and feet appliqués)

2/3 yard white tone-on-tone (appliqué foundations)

7/8 yard backing fabric

29" square batting

Lightweight fusible web

Fine-point permanent fabric marker: black

Finished quilt: 20½" square
Finished blocks: 5" square, 10" square

Cut Fabrics

Cut pieces in the following order. This project uses *Birds of a Feather* patterns on *Pattern Sheet 1.*

To use fusible web for appliquéing, complete the following steps.

1. Lay fusible web, paper side up, over patterns. Use a pencil to trace each pattern the number of times indicated in cutting instructions, leaving ½" between tracings. Cut out each fusible-web shape roughly ¼" outside traced lines.

2. Following manufacturer's instructions, press each fusible-web shape onto wrong side of designated fabric; let cool. Cut out fabric shapes on drawn lines. Peel off paper backings to prepare appliqués.

From multicolor print, cut:
- 3—2½×42" binding strips
- 1 of Pattern A

From assorted bright prints, cut:
- 1 of Pattern B
- 6 *each* of patterns E and E reversed
- 12 of Pattern F

From yellow-and-orange print, cut:
- 1 *each* of patterns C and D
- 12 *each* of patterns G and H

From white tone-on-tone, cut:
- 1—10½" square
- 12—5½" squares

Appliqué Blocks

1. Referring to **Diagram 5**, position multicolor print A bird body, assorted bright print B wing, and yellow-and-orange print C feet and D beak on white tone-on-tone 10½" square. Following manufacturer's directions, fuse pieces in place to make large bird block.

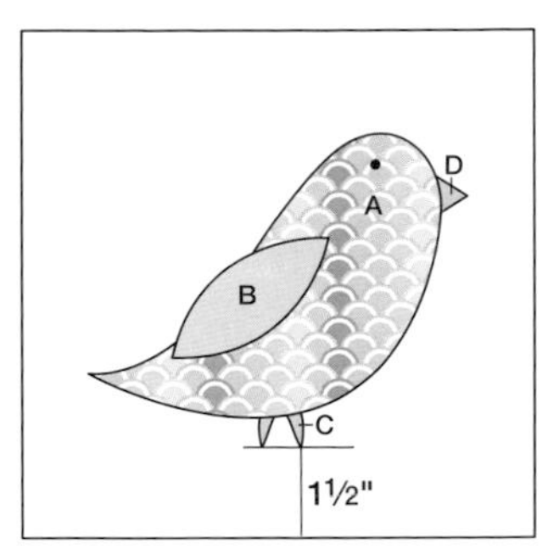

Diagram 5

2. Referring to **Diagram 6,** position assorted bright print E bird body and F wing, and yellow-and-orange print G feet and H beak on a white tone-on-tone 5½" square. Fuse pieces in place as before to make a small bird A block. Repeat to make six small bird A blocks total.

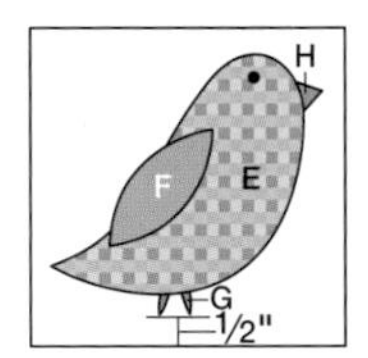

Diagram 6

3. Position assorted bright print E reversed bird body and F wing, and yellow-and-orange print G feet and H beak on a white tone-on-tone 5½" square in a mirror image of **Diagram 6.** Fuse pieces in place as before to make a small bird B block. Repeat to make six small bird B blocks total.

Assemble Quilt Top

1. Referring to photo, *above right,* for placement, lay out large bird block and small bird A and B blocks in three rows. Sew together small bird blocks in middle row; press seams in one direction, then join pieces in each horizontal row. Press seams in one direction, alternating direction with each row.

2. Join rows to complete quilt top. Press seams in one direction.

Finish Quilt

1. Layer quilt top, batting, and backing; baste. (For details, see Complete Quilt, *page 159.*)

2. Quilt as desired. Variegated thread was used to machine-quilt wavy lines through the bird wings and bodies. Orange thread and a small zigzag stitch winds around the bird beaks and feet. A continuous loop in white thread accents the background.

3. Bind with multicolor print binding strips. (For details, see Complete Quilt.)

4. Referring to photo, *above,* for placement, use a fine-point permanent marker to print names and dates of birth. Use marker to draw and fill in a small circle for each bird's eye.

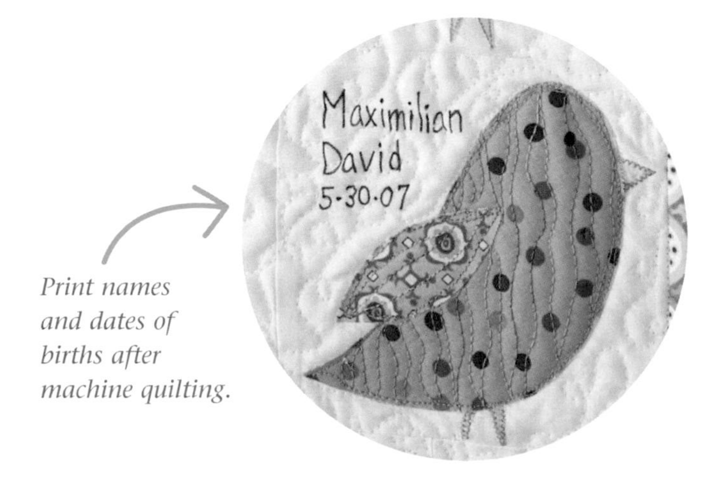

Print names and dates of births after machine quilting.

ARTFULLY *Inspired*

Gardens are often works of art, and designer Kim Diehl captures her view of new spring blooms in this freezer-paper-appliqué table topper. A subtle pieced foundation provides the perfect backdrop for the machine-appliquéd flower design—one that would also look stunning gracing a wall.

Materials

5/8 yard beige print (blocks)

1 1/2 yards cream print (blocks)

1/2 yard green print (stem and leaf appliqués)

9×22" piece (fat eighth) black print (flower center appliqués)

1 1/4 yards red print (flower appliqués, border, binding)

2 3/4 yards backing fabric

49" square batting

Clear monofilament thread

Freezer paper

Fabric glue stick

Finished quilt: 40 1/2" square
Finished block: 8" square

Quantities are for 44/45"-wide, 100% cotton fabrics. **Measurements** include 1/4" seam allowances. Sew with right sides together unless otherwise stated.

Cut Fabrics

Cut pieces in the following order. Patterns are on *Pattern Sheet 1.*

The instructions that follow use a freezer-paper method to prepare pieces for machine appliqué. (Patterns are provided for this technique; if you're using another method, reverse patterns using a light box or sunny window.)

1. Lay freezer paper, shiny side down, over patterns. With a pencil, trace each pattern the number of times indicated in cutting instructions. Cut out freezer-paper shapes on drawn lines.

2. Place a small amount of fabric glue on dull side of freezer-paper shapes; position shapes on wrong sides of designated fabrics, leaving 1/2" between shapes. Cut out each shape, adding a 3/16" seam allowance to all edges. Clip seam allowances of curves as necessary, stopping a thread or two away from freezer paper. Clip inner points just to the paper edge.

3. Beginning on a gently curved edge, use tip of a hot dry iron to press seam allowance of each shape over edge onto shiny side of freezer paper; let cool.

continued

From beige print, cut:
- 64—2½" squares
- 128—1½" squares

From cream print, cut:
- 16—6½" squares
- 64—1½×4½" rectangles
- 64—1½×3½" rectangles

From green print, cut:
- 1—18" square, cutting it into enough 1¼"-wide bias strips to total 185" in length for stem appliqués (For details, see Cut Bias Strips, *page 157.*)
- 32 of Pattern E
- 12 of Pattern D

From black print, cut:
- 17 of Pattern C

From red print, cut:
- 5—2½×42" binding strips
- 2—4½×40½" border strips
- 2—4½×32½" border strips
- 12 of Pattern B
- 4 of Pattern A

Assemble Appliqué Foundation Blocks

1. Use a pencil to mark a diagonal line on wrong side of each beige print 2½" and 1½" square.

2. Align a marked beige print 2½" square with one corner of a cream print 6½" square (**Diagram 1;** note direction of drawn line). Sew on drawn line; trim excess, leaving ¼" seam allowance. Press open attached triangle, pressing seam toward beige print.

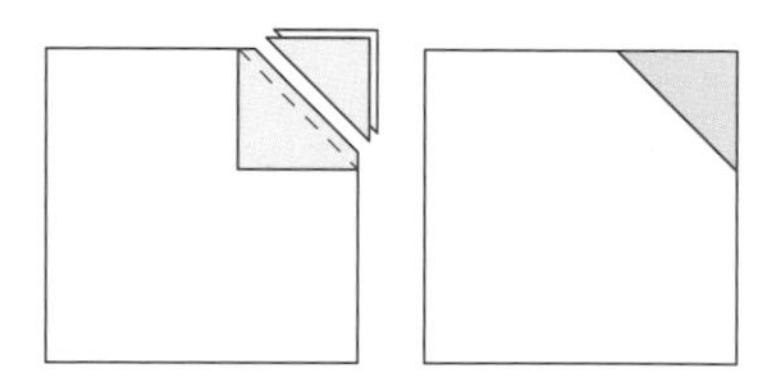

Diagram 1

3. Align a marked beige print 2½" square with each remaining corner (**Diagram 2;** note direction of drawn lines). Stitch, trim, and press as before to make a Snowball unit. The Snowball unit should be 6½" square including seam allowances.

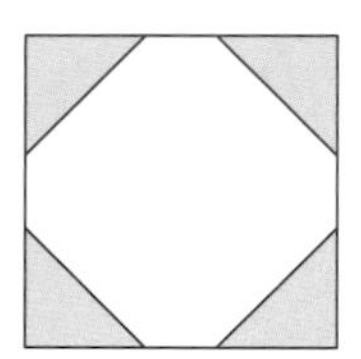

Diagram 2

4. Repeat steps 2 and 3 to make 16 Snowball units total.

5. Align a marked beige print 1½" square with one end of a cream print 1½×3½" rectangle (**Diagram 3;** note direction of drawn line). Stitch on drawn line; trim excess, leaving ¼" seam allowance. Press open attached triangle, pressing seam toward beige print, to make an A rectangle. The A rectangle should be 3½×1½" including seam allowances. Repeat to make 32 A rectangles total.

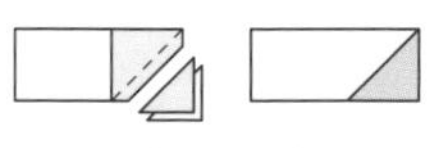

Diagram 3

6. Referring to **Diagram 4**, repeat Step 5 to make 32 B rectangles total (each will be a mirror image of an A rectangle).

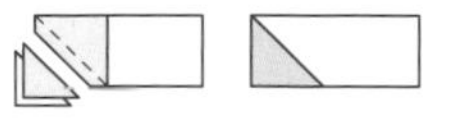

Diagram 4

7. Sew together A and B rectangles to make a short Flying Geese unit **(Diagram 5).** Press seam toward A rectangle. The short Flying Geese unit should be 6½×1½" including seam allowances. Repeat to make 32 short Flying Geese units total.

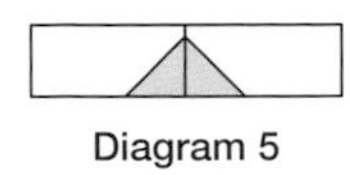

Diagram 5

8. Using marked beige print 1½" squares and cream print 1½×4½" rectangles, repeat steps 5–7 to make 32 long Flying Geese units. Each long Flying Geese unit should be 8½×1½" including seam allowances.

9. Join short Flying Geese units to opposite edges of a Snowball unit **(Diagram 6).** Add long Flying Geese units to remaining edges to make an appliqué foundation block. Press all seams toward Flying Geese units. The block should be 8½" square including seam allowances. Repeat to make 16 appliqué foundation blocks total.

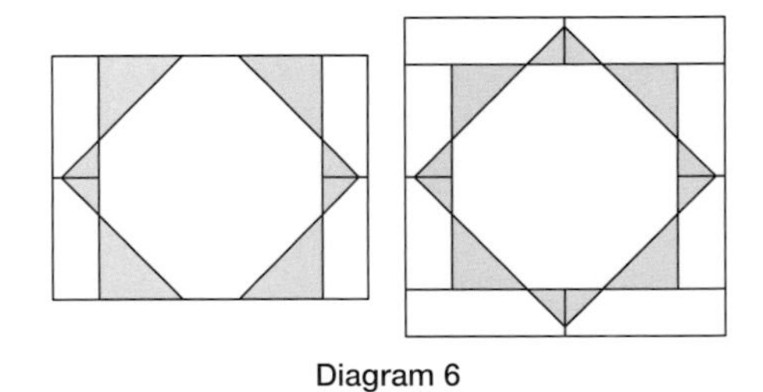

Diagram 6

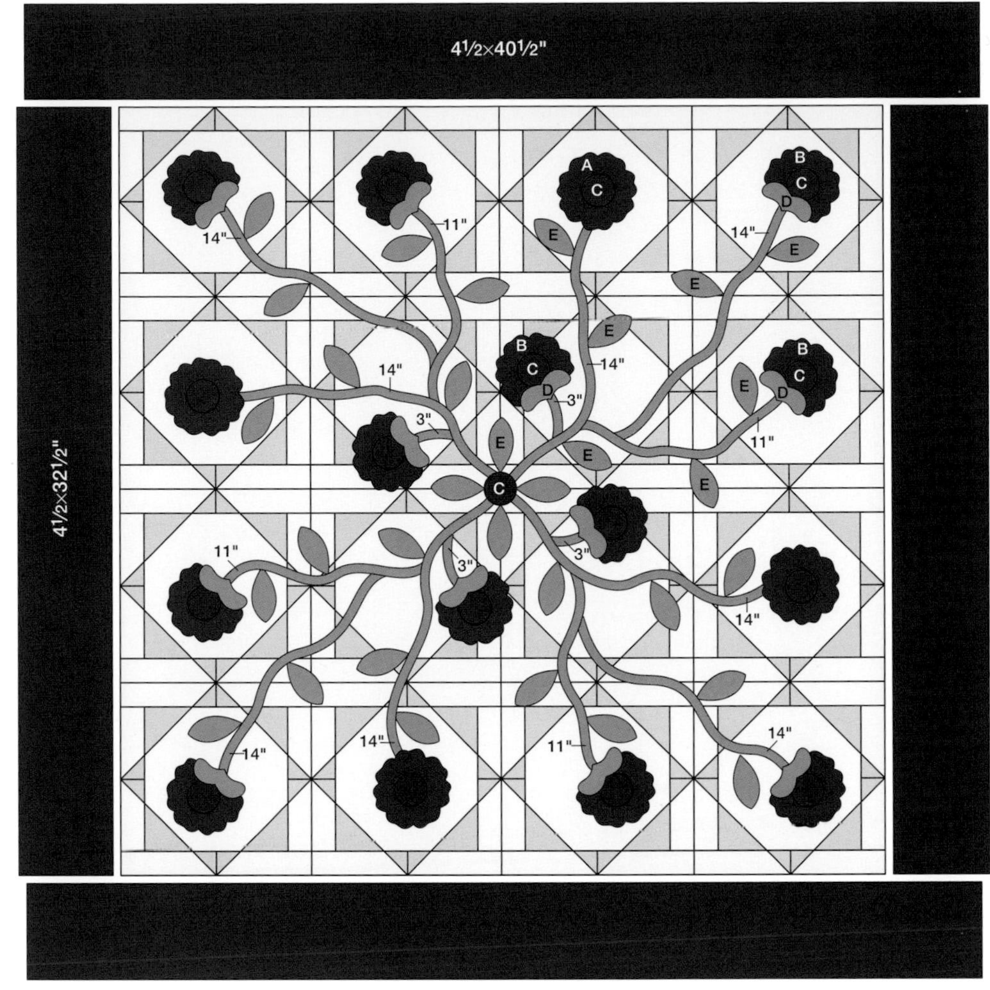

Quilt Assembly Diagram

Assemble Quilt Center

1. Referring to **Quilt Assembly Diagram,** lay out appliqué foundation blocks in four rows.

2. Sew together blocks in each row. Press seams in one direction, alternating direction with each row. Join rows to make quilt center. Press seams in one direction. The quilt center should be 32½" square including seam allowances.

Prepare Stem Appliqués

1. Using diagonal seams, sew together green print 1¼"-wide bias strips to make a 185"-long strip.

2. Fold green print strip in half lengthwise with wrong side inside; press. Stitch a scant ¼" from long edges **(Diagram 7).** Refold strip, centering seam in back; press.

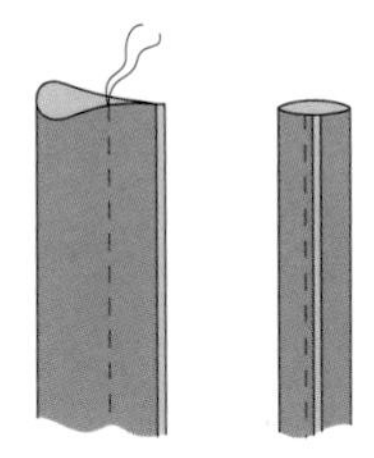

Diagram 7

3. Cut prepared green print strip into:
- 8—14"-long stems
- 4—11"-long stems
- 4—3"-long stems

Appliqué Quilt Center

1. Set up sewing machine with monofilament thread in needle and neutral thread in bobbin. Use a tiny zigzag stitch, so left-hand stitch is 2 to 3 threads inside appliqué edge and right-hand stitch is in foundation fabric, right next to appliqué edge.

2. Referring to **Quilt Assembly Diagram,** arrange stems on quilt center. Tuck under ends as needed. When you are pleased with the arrangement, glue-baste in place.

continued

3. Working from the bottom layer to the top, zigzag-stitch stems in place.

4. Referring to **Quilt Assembly Diagram**, lay out A and B flowers, C flower centers, D calyxes, and E leaves on quilt center. Baste in place.

5. Working from bottom layer to top, machine-zigzag-stitch appliqués in place. To remove freezer-paper shapes, trim away excess foundation fabric from behind appliqués, leaving ¼" seam allowances. With your fingertip, loosen freezer paper and gently peel freezer paper away.

Add Border

Sew short red print border strips to opposite edges of quilt center. Add long red print border strips to remaining edges to complete quilt top. Press all seams toward border.

Finish Quilt

1. Layer quilt top, batting, and backing; baste. (For details, see Complete Quilt, *page 159*.)

2. Quilt as desired. Machine-quilter Celeste Freiberg stitched an overall teardrop motif across the quilt center. A meandering feathered cable adds texture to the border. Using cream-color thread, Kim hand-quilted outline stitches on the flower appliqués.

3. Bind with red print binding strips. (For details, see Complete Quilt.)

FALLING LEAVES

Omit the appliqué and showcase a bounty of leaf prints centered in windowpane-like blocks.

Materials

⅝ yard green print (blocks)

⅞ yard cream tone-on-tone (blocks)

16—6½" squares assorted leaf prints in green, orange, brown, and gold (blocks)

⅝ yard multicolor leaf print (border)

½ yard gold tone-on-tone (binding)

2¾ yards backing fabric

49" square batting

Finished quilt: 40½" square

Cut Fabrics

Cut pieces in the following order.

From green print, cut:
- 64—2½" squares
- 128—1½" squares

From cream tone-on-tone, cut:
- 64—1½×4½" rectangles
- 64—1½×3½" rectangles

From multicolor leaf print, cut:
- 2—4½×40½" border strips
- 2—4½×32½" border strips

From gold tone-on-tone, cut:
- 5—2½×42" binding strips

Assemble Blocks

1. Use a pencil to mark a diagonal line on wrong side of each green print 2½" and 1½" square.

2. Referring to Assemble Appliqué Foundation Blocks, steps 2–9, *pages 150* and *151*, use marked green print 2½" and 1½" squares, assorted leaf print 6½" squares, cream tone-on-tone 1½×3½" rectangles, and cream tone-on-tone 1½×4½" rectangles to make 16 blocks total.

continued

Assemble Quilt Center

1. Referring to **Quilt Assembly Diagram**, lay out blocks in four rows.

2. Sew together blocks in each row. Press seams in one direction, alternating direction with each row. Join rows to make quilt center. Press seams in one direction. The quilt center should be 32½" square including seam allowances.

Add Border

Sew short multicolor leaf print border strips to opposite edges of quilt center. Add long leaf print border strips to remaining edges to complete quilt top. Press all seams toward border.

Finish Quilt

1. Layer quilt top, batting, and backing; baste. (For details, see Complete Quilt, *page 159*.)

2. Quilt as desired. The featured quilt is stitched with a continuous leaf-and-vine design.

3. Bind with gold tone-on-tone binding strips. (For details, see Complete Quilt.)

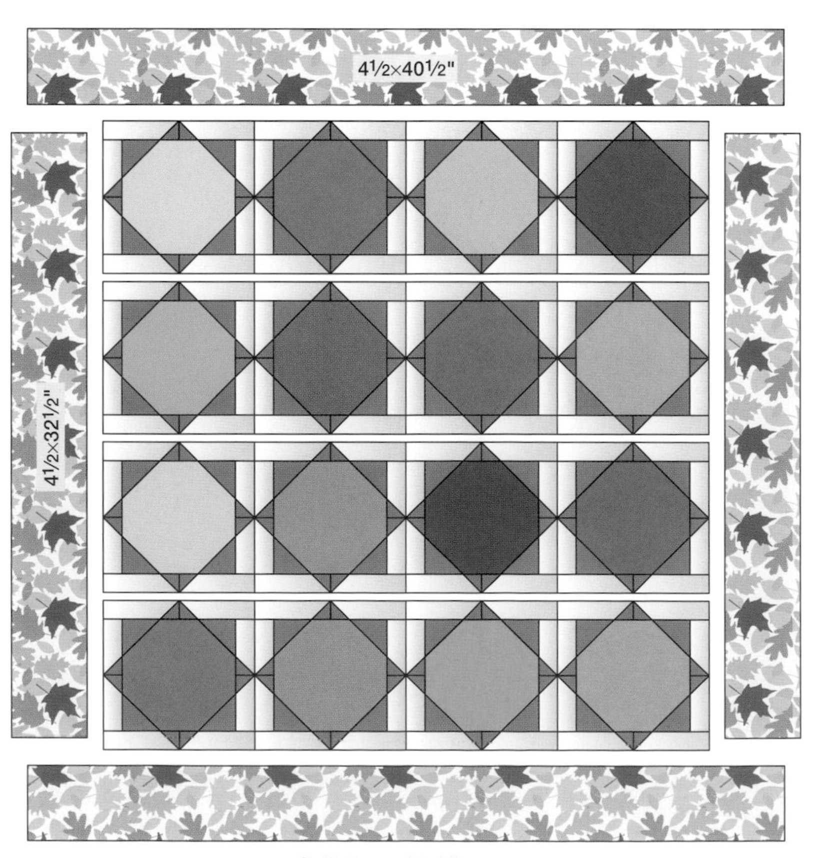

Quilt Assembly Diagram

CIRCLES SEWING BAG

Use a single appliqué shape from Artfully Inspired *to adorn a take-along sewing kit.*

Materials

Scraps of green, brown, and aqua prints (appliqués)

9×22" piece (fat eighth) cream print (bag body, lining)

Freezer paper

Fabric glue stick

9"-long zipper: cream

Finished bag: 7½×4"

Cut Fabrics

Cut pieces in the following order.

This project uses *Artfully Inspired* Pattern C on *Pattern Sheet 1*. To use a freezer-paper method to prepare C circles for hand appliqué, refer to Cut Fabrics, steps 1–3, *page 149*.

From *each* green, brown, and aqua scrap, cut:
- 1 of Pattern C

From cream print, cut:
- 4—4½×8" rectangles for bag body and lining

continued

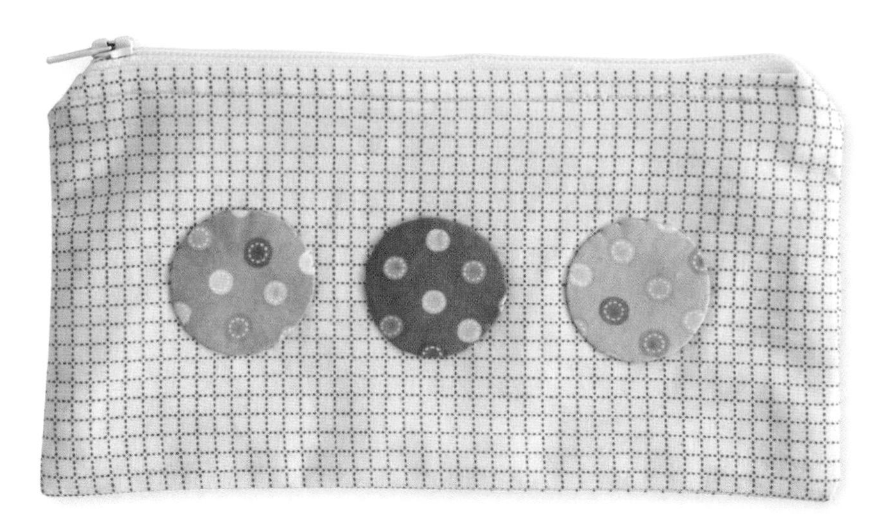

Appliqué Circles

1. Remove freezer paper from prepared C circle appliqués.

2. Referring to **Appliqué Placement Diagram**, arrange circle appliqués on a cream print 8×4½" rectangle; glue-baste in place.

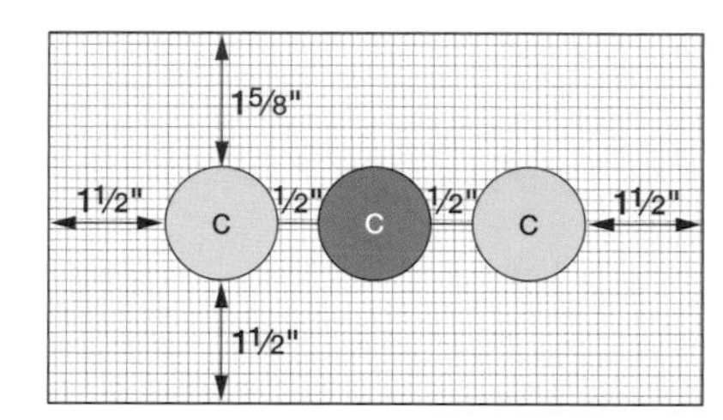

Appliqué Placement Diagram

3. Using small slip stitches, hand-appliqué circles in place to make bag body front.

Assemble Bag

1. Place a cream print 8×4½" lining rectangle, right side up, on a flat surface. Center and align cream zipper faceup along long edge of rectangle. Place bag body front facedown on top of zipper; pin together through all three layers.

2. Using a zipper foot and a ¼" seam allowance, stitch layers together **(Diagram 8)**.

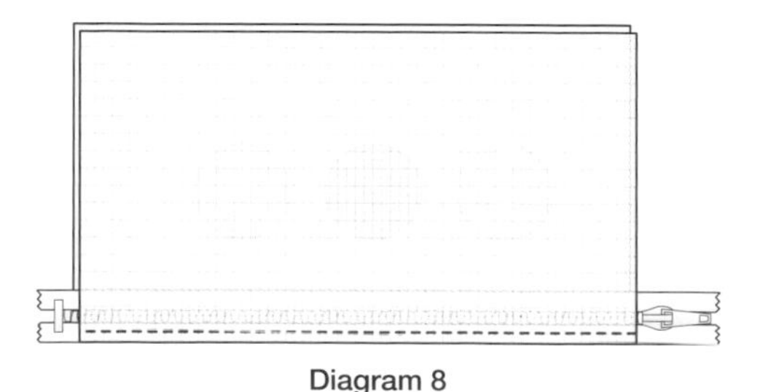

Diagram 8

3. Finger-press bag body front and lining away from zipper. Topstitch a scant ¼" from fold to make front unit **(Diagram 9)**.

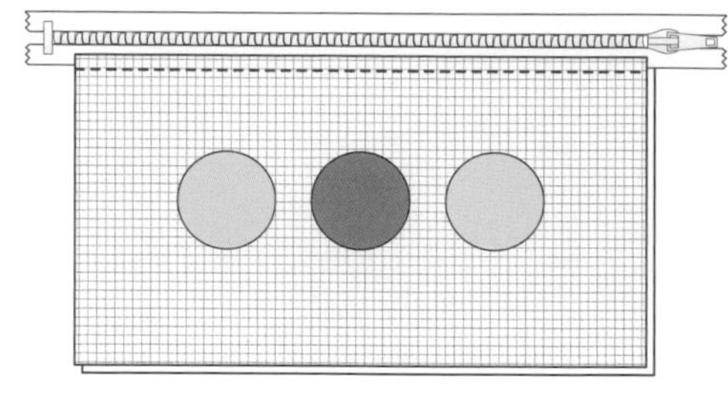

Diagram 9

4. Using remaining cream print 8×4½" rectangles, repeat steps 1–3 to stitch remaining zipper edge and make back unit.

5. Move zipper tab to center of zipper.

6. Open up front unit and back unit. With right sides together, layer front and back units so bag body front and back are together and lining front and back are together; pin. Join units around all edges, leaving a 3" opening along lining edge for turning **(Diagram 10)**.

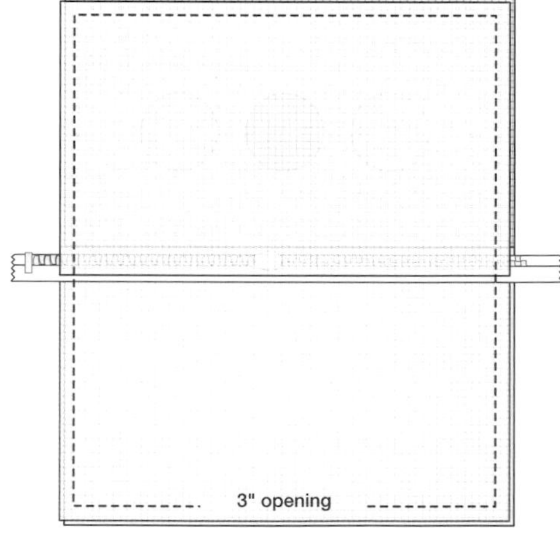

Diagram 10

7. Turn units right side out through opening and finger-press seams. Slip-stitch lining opening closed. Insert lining into bag body to complete bag.

QUILTER'S SCHOOLHOUSE

Refer to these tips and techniques when making your projects.

CHOOSE FABRICS

The best fabric for quiltmaking is 100% cotton because it minimizes seam distortion, presses crisply, and is easy to quilt. Unless otherwise noted, quantities in Materials lists are for 44/45"-wide fabrics. We call for a little extra yardage to allow for minor errors and slight shrinkage.

CUT BIAS STRIPS

Strips for curved appliqué pattern pieces, such as meandering vines, and for binding curved edges should be cut on the bias, which runs at a 45° angle to the selvages of a woven fabric and has the most give or stretch.

To cut bias strips, begin with a fabric square or rectangle. Use a large acrylic ruler to square up the left edge of the fabric. Then make a cut at a 45° angle to the left edge **(Bias Strip Diagram).** Handle the diagonal edges carefully to avoid distorting the bias. To cut a strip, measure the desired width parallel to the 45° cut edge; cut. Continue cutting enough strips to total the length needed.

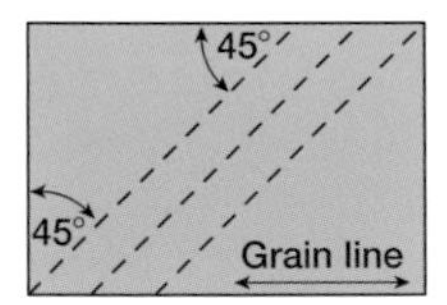

Bias Strip Diagram

MAKE AND USE TEMPLATES

Make Templates

A template is a pattern made from extra-sturdy material so you can trace around it many times without wearing away the edges. Acrylic templates for many common shapes are available at quilt shops. Or make your own templates by duplicating printed patterns (such as those on the Pattern Sheet) onto template plastic.

To make permanent templates, we recommend using easy-to-cut template plastic. This material lasts indefinitely, and its transparency allows you to trace the pattern directly onto its surface.

To make a template, lay the plastic over a printed pattern. Trace the pattern onto the plastic using a ruler and a permanent marker to ensure straight lines, accurate corners, and permanency.

For hand piecing and appliqué, make templates the exact size the finished pieces will be (without seam allowances). For hand piecing, this means tracing the patterns' dashed lines.

For machine piecing, make templates that include seam allowances by tracing the patterns' solid and dashed lines.

For easy reference, mark each template with its letter designation, grain line (if noted on the pattern), and block name. Cut out the traced shapes on their outer lines. Verify each template's shape and size by placing it over its printed pattern. Templates must be accurate because errors, however small, will compound many times as you assemble a quilt. To check the templates' accuracy, make a test block before cutting the fabric pieces for an entire quilt.

Use Templates

To trace a template on fabric, use a pencil, a white dressmaker's pencil, chalk, or a special fabric marker that makes a thin, accurate line. Do not use a ballpoint or ink pen; it may bleed if washed. Test all marking tools on a fabric scrap before using them.

To make pieces for hand piecing or appliqué, place a template facedown on the wrong side of the fabric and trace. Then reposition the template at least ½" away from the previous tracing, trace again, and repeat **(Diagram 1).**

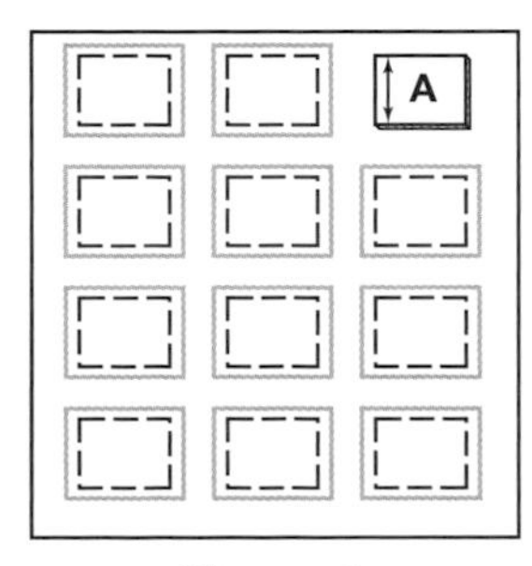

Diagram 1

The lines you trace on the fabric are sewing lines. Mark cutting lines ¼" away from the sewing lines, or estimate the distance by eye when cutting out the pieces with scissors. For hand piecing, add a ¼" seam allowance; for hand appliqué, add a 3/16" seam allowance.

Because templates used to make pieces for machine piecing have seam allowances included, you can use common tracing lines for efficient cutting. Place a template facedown on the wrong side of the fabric, and trace. Then reposition the template without a space between it and the previous tracing, trace again, and repeat **(Diagram 2).** Using a rotary cutter and ruler, cut out pieces, cutting precisely on the drawn lines.

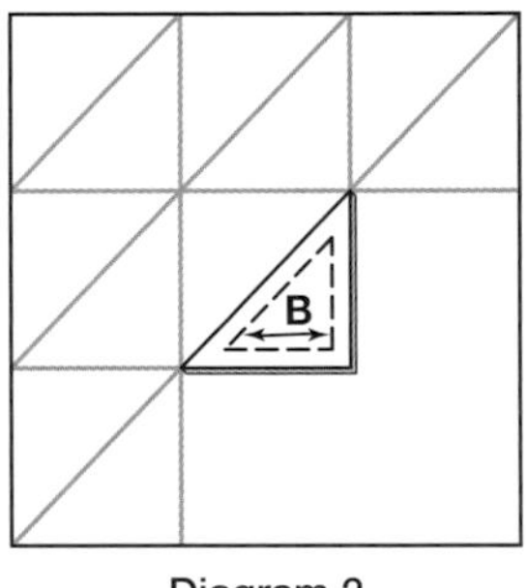

Diagram 2

PIECING

Hand Piecing

In hand piecing, seams are sewn only on the marked sewing lines; the seam allowances remain unstitched. Begin by matching the edges of two pieces with the fabrics' right sides together. Sewing lines should be marked on the wrong side of each piece. Push a pin through both fabric layers at each corner (**Diagram 3,** *page 158*). Secure the pins perpendicular to the sewing line. Insert more pins between the corners.

Insert a needle through both fabrics at the seam-line corner. Make one or two backstitches atop the first stitch to secure the thread. Weave the needle in and out of the fabric along the seam line, taking four to six tiny stitches at

continued

a time before you pull the thread taut **(Diagram 4).** Remove the pins as you sew. Turn the work over occasionally to see that the stitching follows the marked sewing line on the other side.

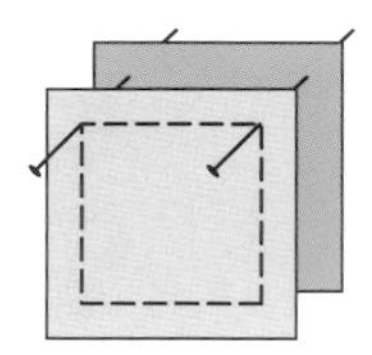
Diagram 3

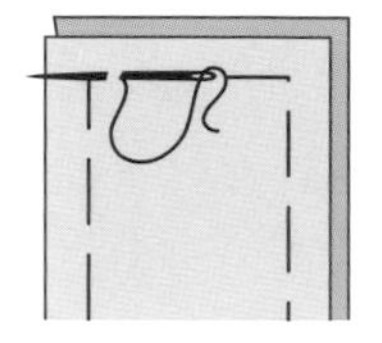
Diagram 4

Sew eight to 10 stitches per inch along the seam line. At the end of the seam, remove the last pin and make the ending stitch through the hole left by the corner pin. Backstitch over the last stitch and end the seam with a loop knot **(Diagram 5).**

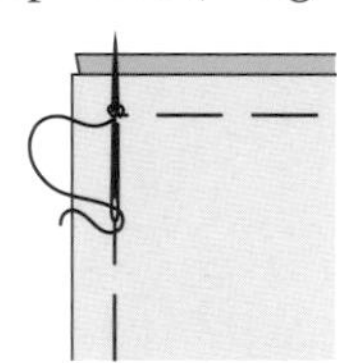
Diagram 5

To join rows of patchwork by hand, hold the sewn pieces with right sides together and seams matched. Insert pins at the corners of the matching pieces. Add additional pins as necessary, securing each pin perpendicular to the sewing line **(Diagram 6).**

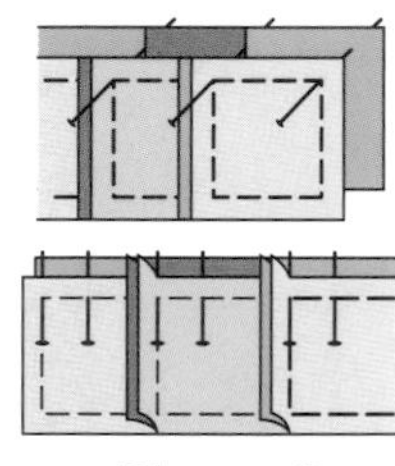
Diagram 6

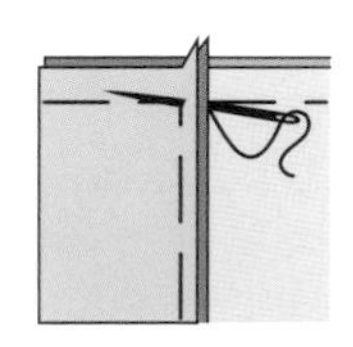
Diagram 7

Stitch the joining seam as before, but do not sew across the seam allowances that join the patches. At each seam allowance, make a backstitch or loop knot; then slide the needle through the seam allowance **(Diagram 7).** Knot or backstitch again to give the intersection strength; then sew the remainder of the seam. Press each seam as it is completed.

Machine Piecing

Machine piecing depends on sewing an exact ¼" seam allowance. Some machines have a presser foot that is the proper width, or a ¼" foot is available. To check the width of a machine's presser foot, sew a sample seam with the raw fabric edges aligned with the right edge of the presser foot; measure the resultant seam allowance using graph paper with a ¼" grid.

Using two thread colors—one in the needle and one in the bobbin—can help you to better match your thread color to your fabrics. If your quilt has many fabrics, use a neutral color, such as gray or beige, for both the top and bobbin threads throughout the quilt.

Press for Success

In quilting, almost every seam needs to be pressed before the piece is sewn to another, so keep your iron and ironing board near your sewing area. It's important to remember to press with an up-and-down motion. Moving the iron around on the fabric can distort seams, especially those sewn on the bias.

Project instructions in this book generally tell you in what direction to press each seam. When in doubt, press the seam allowance toward the darker fabric. When joining rows of blocks, alternate the direction the seam allowances are pressed to ensure flat corners.

Set in Pieces

The key to sewing angled pieces together is aligning marked matching points carefully. Whether you're stitching by machine or hand, start and stop sewing precisely at the matching points (see dots in **Diagram 8**, top) and backstitch to secure the ends of the seams. This prepares the angle for the next piece to be set in.

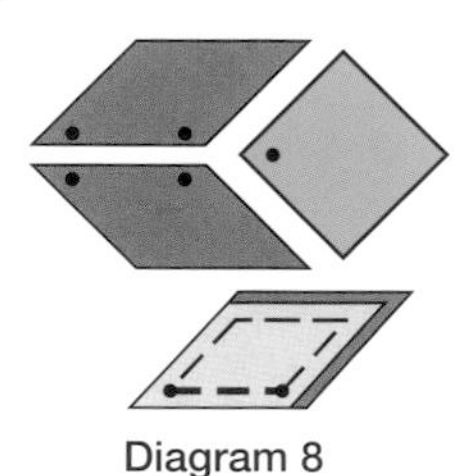
Diagram 8

Join two diamond pieces, sewing between matching points to make an angled unit **(Diagram 8).**

Follow the specific instructions for either machine or hand piecing to complete the set-in seam.

MACHINE PIECING

With right sides together, pin one piece of the angled unit to one edge of the square **(Diagram 9).** Match the seam's matching points by pushing a pin through both fabric layers to check the alignment. Machine-stitch the seam between the matching points. Backstitch to secure the ends of the seam; do not stitch into the ¼" seam allowance. Remove the unit from the sewing machine.

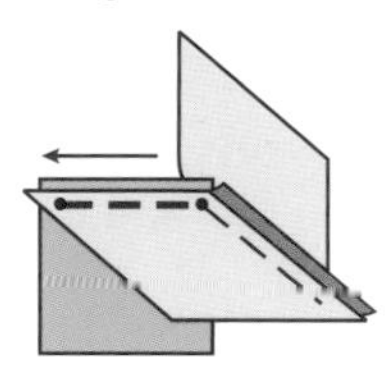
Diagram 9

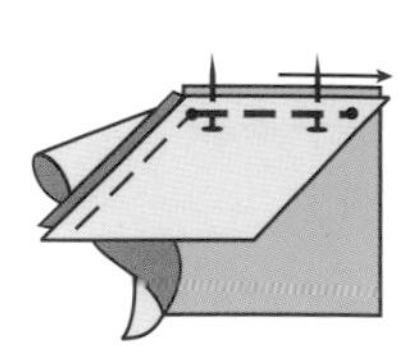
Diagram 10

Bring the adjacent edge of the angled unit up and align it with the next edge of the square **(Diagram 10).** Insert a pin in each corner to align matching points; then pin the remainder of the seam. Machine-stitch between matching points as before. Press the seam allowances of the set-in piece away from it.

HAND PIECING

Pin one piece of the angled unit to one edge of the square with right sides together **(Diagram 11).** Use pins to align matching points at the corners.

Hand-sew the seam from the open end of the angle into the corner. Remove pins as you sew between matching points. Backstitch at the corner to secure stitches. Do not sew into the ¼" seam allowance, and do not cut your thread.

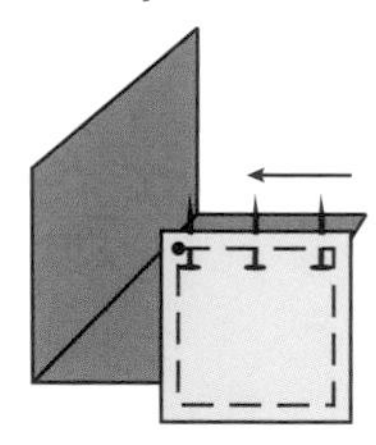
Diagram 11

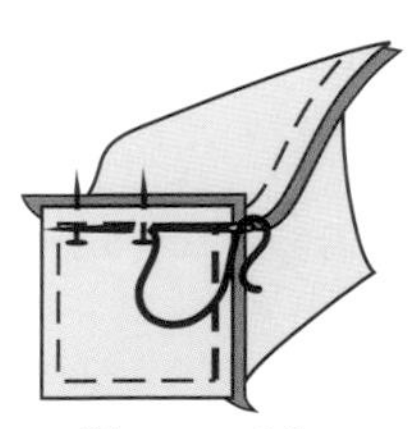
Diagram 12

Bring the adjacent edge of the square up, and align it with the other edge of the angled unit. Insert a pin in each corner to align matching points; then pin the remainder of the seam **(Diagram 12).** Continuing the thread from the previous seam, hand-sew the seam from the corner to the open end of the angle, removing pins as you sew. Press the seam allowances of the set-in piece away from it.

MITER BORDERS

A border surrounds the piecework of many quilts. Mitered corners add to a border's frame effect.

To add a border with mitered corners, first pin a border strip to a quilt top edge, matching the center of the strip and the center of the quilt top edge. Allow excess border fabric to extend beyond the edges. Sew together, beginning and ending the seam ¼" from the quilt top corners **(Diagram 13).** Repeat with the remaining border strips. Press the seam allowances toward the border strips.

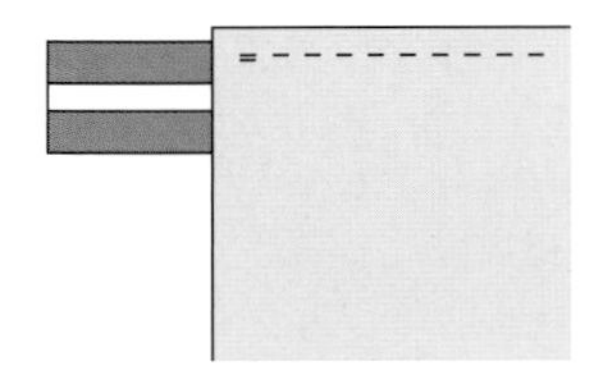

Diagram 13

Overlap the border strips at each corner **(Diagram 14).** Align the edge of a 90° right triangle with the raw edge of a top border strip so the long edge of the triangle intersects the seam in the corner. With a pencil, draw along the edge of the triangle from the border seam out to the raw edge. Place the bottom border strip on top, and repeat the marking process.

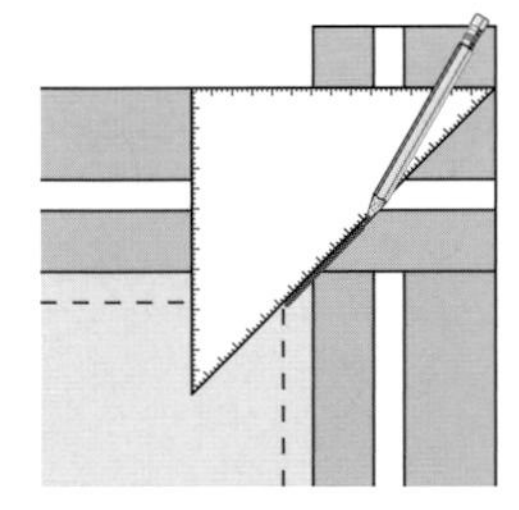

Diagram 14

With the right sides of adjacent border strips together, match the marked seam lines and pin **(Diagram 15).**

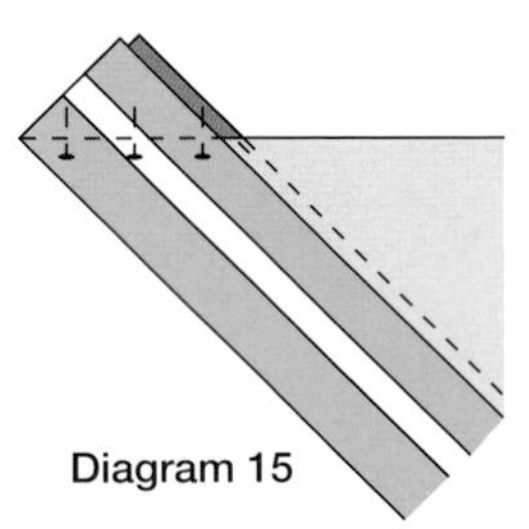

Diagram 15

Beginning with a backstitch at the inside corner, stitch exactly on the marked lines to the outside edges of the border strips. Check the right side of the corner to see that it lies flat. Then trim the excess fabric, leaving a ¼" seam allowance. Press the seam open. Mark and sew the remaining corners in the same manner.

COMPLETE QUILT

Layering

Cut and piece backing fabric to measure at least 4" bigger on all sides than the quilt top. Press seams open. With wrong sides together, layer quilt top and backing fabric with the batting in between; baste. Quilt as desired.

Binding

Binding for most quilts is cut on the straight grain of the fabric. If your quilt has curved edges, cut the strips on the bias (see *page 157*). Cutting instructions for projects in this book specify the number of binding strips or a total length needed to finish the quilt. The instructions also specify enough width for a French-fold, or double-layer, binding because it's easier to apply and adds durability.

Join strips with diagonal seams to make one continuous binding strip **(Diagram 16).** Trim excess fabric, leaving ¼" seam allowances. Press seams open. Fold one end of the binding strip under 1" **(Diagram 17)**; press. With wrong side inside, fold strip in half lengthwise and press **(Diagram 18).**

Beginning in the center of one edge, place binding strip against right side of quilt top, aligning binding strip's raw edges with quilt top's raw edge **(Diagram 19).** Beginning 1½" from the folded edge, sew through all layers, stopping ¼" from the corner. Backstitch; then clip threads. Remove quilt from under presser foot.

Fold binding strip upward **(Diagram 20)**, creating a diagonal fold, and finger-press.

Holding diagonal fold in place with your finger, bring binding strip down in line with next edge of quilt top, making a horizontal fold that aligns with the quilt edge **(Diagram 21).**

Start sewing again at top of horizontal fold, stitching through all layers. Sew around quilt, turning each corner in the same manner.

When you return to starting point, encase binding strip's raw edge inside the folded end **(Diagram 22).** Finish sewing to starting point **(Diagram 23).** Trim batting and backing fabric even with quilt top edges.

Turn the binding over the edge to the back. Hand-stitch binding to backing fabric, making sure to cover all machine stitching.

To make mitered corners on the back, hand-stitch up to a corner; fold miter in the binding. Take a stitch or two into the fold to secure it. Then stitch the binding in place up to the next corner. Finish each corner in the same manner.

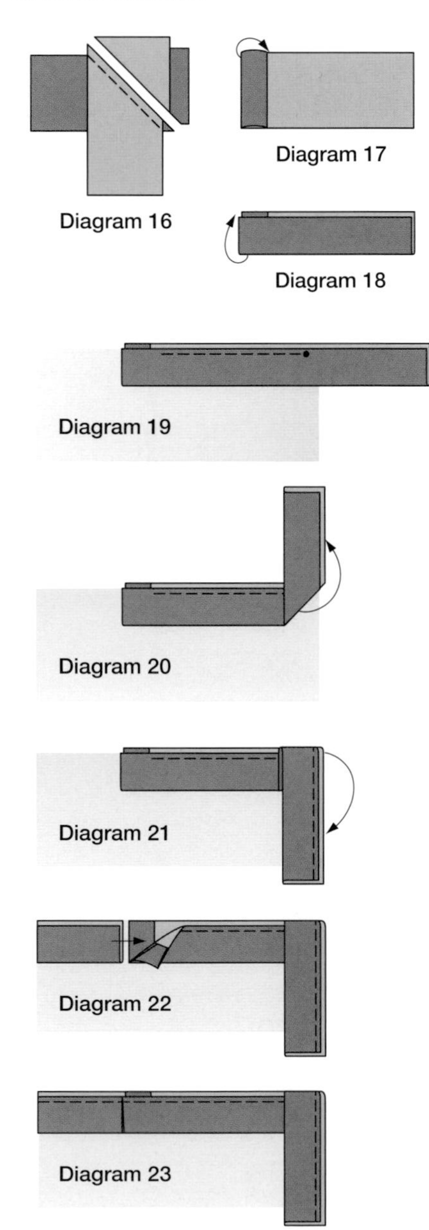

Diagram 16

Diagram 17

Diagram 18

Diagram 19

Diagram 20

Diagram 21

Diagram 22

Diagram 23

CREDITS

Quilt Designers

Color Burst
Angela Blair and Amy Fuehrer

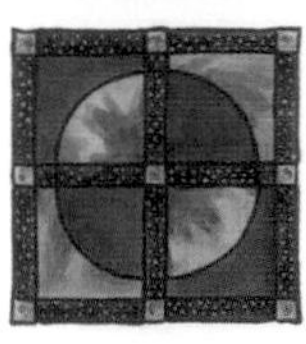

Ring of Fire
Barbara Brackman
barbarabrackman.com

Artfully Inspired, Cabin Cozy
Kim Diehl
kimdiehl.com

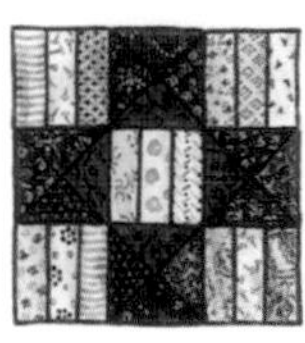

Rhythm & Blues
Monique Dillard
of Open Gate Quilts
opengatequilts.com

Flying Solo, Summer Breeze
Julie Hendricksen
of JJ Stitches
jjstitches.com

Budding Beauty
Linda Hohag
of Brandywine Design
brandywine-design.com

Birds of a Feather
Kevin Kosbab
of Feed Dog Designs
feeddog.net

Nantucket Stars
Miriam Kujac
Quilt collector

Midnight Garden
Jo Morton
jomortonquilts.com

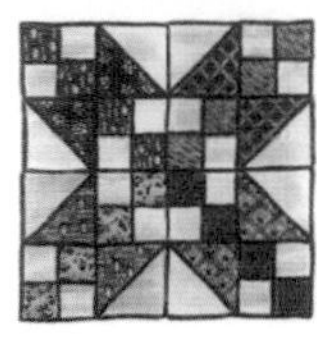

Pick & Choose
Carrie Nelson
of Miss Rosie's Quilt Co.
missrosiesquiltco.com

Modern Mix
Mabeth Oxenreider

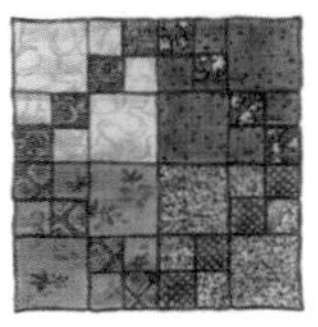

Walled Garden
Sheila Sinclair Snyder

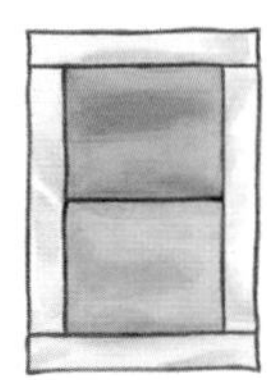

Color Cues
Amy Walsh
of Blue Underground Studios
blueundergroundstudios.com

Laura Boehnke, *Quilt Tester*
With a keen color sense and an astute use of fabrics, Laura tests each project in *American Patchwork & Quilting®* magazine by making at least four blocks.

Project Makers & Quilters
Jody Sanders: pages 13, 46, 107, 125, 127, 136, 138, 155
Laura Boehnke: pages 14, 33, 77, 116
Nancy Sharr: page 14
Kathleen Williams: page 21
Mary Lynn Siefken: page 21
Janelle Swenson: pages 24, 53, 118
Cindy Tolliver: pages 33, 53, 125, 153
Mary Pepper: pages 34, 44
Kat Tichenor: page 55
Jan Ragaller: pages 63, 75
Kelly Edwards: pages 63, 75
Peggy Bruns: page 66
Sue Urich: page 77
Jill Abeloe Mead: page 84
Karen Gilson: page 84
Elizabeth Tisinger Beese: pages 86, 147
Marilyn Cox: page 94
Ilene Jennings: page 97
Monique Dillard: page 108
LeAnne Olson: page 108
Jennifer Erbe Keltner: page 144
Joan Gelder: page 153

Materials Suppliers
Andover Fabrics
Benartex
Cherrywood Fabrics
Hoffman California Fabrics
In the Beginning Fabrics
May Arts
Michael Miller Fabrics
Moda Fabrics
Northcott Silk
P&B Textiles
Paintbrush Studio for Fabri-Quilt
Red Rooster Fabrics
Riley Blake Designs
RJR Fabrics
Robert Kaufman Fabrics
Rowan Fabrics
Timeless Treasures Fabrics

Photographers
Adam Albright: pages 21, 24, 34, 44, 59, 116, 118, 144
King Au: page 9
Marty Baldwin: pages 13, 55, 127, 136, 138
Jason Donnelly: pages 147, 155
Kathryn Gamble: pages 81, 86, 120
Cameron Sadeghpour: pages 14, 26, 77, 100, 110, 130, 148
Greg Scheidemann: pages 17, 33, 46, 53, 63, 66, 71, 75, 84, 88, 94, 97, 107, 108, 125, 141, 153
Perry Struse: pages 38, 48